WANDERING
IN THE
WILDERNESS

i

WANDERING IN THE WILDERNESS

Changes and Challenges to Emerging Adults' Christian Faith

Brian Simmons

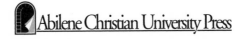
Abilene Christian University Press

WANDERING IN THE WILDERNESS
CHANGES AND CHALLENGES TO EMERGING ADULTS' CHRISTIAN FAITH

ACU
PRESS

Copyright 2011 by Brian Simmons

ISBN 978-0-89112-285-2
LCCN 2011009557

Printed in the United States of America

LIBRARY OF CONGRESS CATALOGING-IN-PUBLICATION DATA
Simmons, Brian, 1964-
 Wandering in the wilderness : changes and challenges to emerging adults' Christian faith / Brian Simmons.
    p. cm.
 Includes bibliographical references.
 ISBN 978-0-89112-285-2
1. Young adults--Religious life--United States. 2. Church work with young adults--United States.
I. Title.
 BV639.Y7S56 2011
 259'.250973--dc22

                                                                                    2011009557

Cover design by Rick Gibson
Interior text design by Sandy Armstrong

For information contact:
Abilene Christian University Press
1626 Campus Court
Abilene, Texas 79601

1-877-816-4455 toll free
www.abilenechristianuniversitypress.com

11 12 13 14 15 16 / 7 6 5 4 3 2 1

To all of my current and former students.
May they never wander in the wilderness.

Contents

Emerging Adults: The Forgotten Group

"We don't even have a name!" That's the part of our conversation that I remember the most. It was one of those phrases that stick out in your mind because it so succinctly captures an idea.

I was seated on a drab spring day in an uncomfortable booth at my favorite fast-food eatery. Across from me sat one of my former students who was a few years removed from her years in college. As a student in my classes, she was successful and confident, thriving in an atmosphere that encouraged her to deepen her faith and explore the intellectual world. However, the slightly disheveled person sitting across from me picking at her burrito was anxious. In an odd way, she seemed beaten down.

We were talking about recent developments in her life and, as was often the case, I turned the conversation toward the topic of her religious faith. "So, how's your spiritual life?" I ventured. "It's Good. . . . Fine. . . . Okay, I guess," she replied.

"That doesn't sound too convincing," I said quietly.

With a heavy sigh, she looked away, put down her barely eaten burrito and launched into a thirty-five-minute tale describing the meandering journey of her religious faith. The story she told me was her version of an identical story I have heard many times over the past two decades that I have been a college professor. It was a story of a once rock-solid religious faith that was now filled with questions and doubts. It was a story of an almost

schizophrenic yearning for real Christian community and a deep disillusion-
ment with the church. It was a story of a child who had drifted away from,
but not abandoned her Savior. Jesus, who had once been a companion, was
now a stranger. Church attendance and involvement that had once come
naturally and filled her calendar were now long abandoned artifacts from
another life. And, toward the end of her distressing story, she spoke the
phrase that opened my eyes to so many things.

"We don't even have a name!"

She continued: "You know, when you're in high school and in the youth
group and all of that, the people at church call you 'The Teens' or 'The Youth
Group' or something like that. And after high school they call you 'College
Students' even if you don't go to college. But what about after college?
What about when you're twenty-five and you're not married? They can't
call you 'Young Marrieds' because not everyone is married. They could call
us 'Singles' but that's sort of demeaning, like something is wrong with you
or like you're 'on the market.' One church calls us 'Young Professionals,'
but that's awkward because nobody I know feels 'professional' and besides,
what does that mean anyway? Maybe that's our problem. We don't even
have a name!"

This book is about the religious faith of people who are between their
twentieth and twenty-ninth birthday. It may be a somewhat uncomfortable
book because it explores the struggles that many people at this place in life
have with religious faith and church. It's an attempt to open a window into
their hearts and minds and see what's there. Some of what's there is hopeful
and encouraging; some is disheartening and sad. It all starts with a name,
or the lack thereof.

Emerging Adults?

Names matter. Communication scholar Julia Wood writes about the
communicative power of labels, noting that humans use labels as a way of
classifying things so as to make sense out of them. Labels (or in this case,
names) place one thing in relation to another and inform us as to what to

expect from a thing carrying a particular label. For example, the recent trend is to use the term "Girls" to refer to female high school basketball teams while using the term "Women's" to refer to college basketball teams. The difference in names reflects the intentional desire to communicate something about the age or maturity of those involved in the activity. Christians ought to understand this for they frequently use labels to help understand the world and distinguish one thing from another. And, choosing one label or name over another always indicates choosing one meaning over another. There are labels for people (e.g. "saved" and "lost"), labels for places (e.g. "auditorium" and "sanctuary"), and labels for roles (e.g. "minister" or "pastor").

What name do you use to identify Christians who are in their twenties? They're not teenagers anymore, so "teenagers" or "adolescents" aren't accurate. They've long since outgrown the high school youth group, so "youth group" is obviously out. Many either never went to or have graduated from college, so "college students" is out too. "Singles" accurately describes many of them, but isn't it a little bit uncomfortable to be classified according to your marital status? In fact, I know many people who loath being identified as single because it so often carries a negative connotation.

I propose calling them "emerging adults." The title defines people by what's going on in their development as people, rather than defining them by age, marital status, or place at church. This title reflects the idea people in their twenties are well on their way to being fully adult but are not quite there yet. During this time of life they experience living on their own and freedom from parental constraints when they reach their twenties. Many also find that with their first "real job" they have more disposable income than at any previous point in their lives. Many of them move away from their hometown and find themselves in new places full of exciting possibilities. They make good and bad choices. Yet they don't yet carry the full responsibilities of adult life. They're typically not yet married and don't have children. There are fewer bills to pay and less is expected of them. They are emerging adults—shedding the motifs of adolescence, working their way toward full adulthood which still lies ahead in the future. I admit that the term "emerging adults" feels a bit technical and cumbersome. It certainly hasn't caught on anywhere outside of academia. But it seems to be the best we can do.

The number of Christian emerging adults is significant. According to the Pew Foundation's 2007 *Religious Landscape Survey*, about 17% of all American Protestants are between the ages of eighteen and twenty-nine. Though not the largest proportion of believers, that's still approximately twenty-seven million people. However, if you think the emerging adults' numerical size doesn't warrant attention, consider this: Most Christians know some Christians in their twenties. They might be your children or your grandchildren. Maybe they're your friends' children. They might be members of your church. You could be in your twenties as you read this book. Of course, anyone thirty or older has lived through the twenties and therefore has first-hand experience with that time of life! As someone at church recently said to me after completing a conversation with several twenties, "I remember what it was like to be their age. They need all the prayer they can get!"

The Group Nobody Talks About

Given emerging adults' relevancy, you would think that their religious faith would be a common topic of conversation. Ironically, it is not. In fact, emerging adults are in many ways the most overlooked group in all of American Christianity. One way to see this is to ask the question, "How many resources are dedicated to different groups of people within the church?" Pre-adolescent children have no small amount of time and energy directed toward their spiritual development. Sunday school classes, vacation Bible schools, children's ministers, leadership training programs, and a plethora of age-specific instructional materials are designed and implemented to "train up a child in the way he should go," as Proverbs 22:6 says. There are highly developed bodies of knowledge for children's Christian education and a myriad of books and Web sites on how to raise Christian children. And, academic researchers have completed numerous studies on the development of children's religious faith.

Even more attention is paid to those in junior and senior high school (typically ages 13-18). In addition to age-specific classes at church, youth ministers are common, often overseeing extensive programs geared toward meeting adolescents' spiritual and social needs. If you were to walk into a Christian bookstore or troll the World Wide Web you would easily find all sorts of people talking about the religious life and faith of adolescents. Amazon.com lists over 3,300 books on youth ministry alone. In fact, it's safe to say that more books have been written in the past twenty years on how to minister to teens than perhaps any other group within the church. The academic study of Christian teens has also expanded as over the past twenty-five years scholars have extensively researched the development of faith among adolescents.

Skipping ahead in the lifecycle, churches also focus a lot of attention on "families" (usually loosely defined as anybody between high school and retirement that is either married or married with children). Many churches have begun to employ family ministers who develop programs of instruction and activity for family units. In fact, it has been noted that "family minister" is the fastest growing ministry title of the past decade. Whether it is marriage enrichment programs, parenting classes, intergenerational activities, or marital counseling, more and more is offered for Christians in this segment of life. More will be said about emerging adults, marriage, and church later. But for now suffice it to say that churches are almost universally more family-focused than they are emerging adult-focused.

Sandwiched between the juggernaut of emphasis on children/teens and the sprawling emphasis on families, emerging adults are usually overlooked. There are far fewer age-specific classes for them at church. Few churches have formal programs designed to meet their spiritual and social needs. While there are some employed to minister to twenties, there are far fewer of them than there are youth or children's ministers. The diversity of titles alone suggests an area in disarray, for some are called "singles ministers" others "young adult ministers" and a few "college ministers." There's even a lively discussion on the internet among these ministers as to *what* to call their ministries; that isn't the case with youth or children's ministries!

The notion of a "singles ministry" is a tricky one. While well-intentioned, some see it as carrying a negative stigma. It's telling that I have never encountered anyone who attached a negative stigma to a ministry program geared toward teens or families, yet I have met many who do so toward programs titled "Singles Ministry." An emerging adult I talked with said, "I hate being referred to as 'a single.' It makes it sound like I'm broken or that there's something wrong with me because I'm not married." Another complained, "There is a singles ministry at my church, but I don't do anything with it. It's basically just a bunch of people looking for someone to marry."

Another common program for emerging adults is the many vibrant ministries to college students. Often based on large college campuses at state universities or in smaller Christian schools, these programs are centered on the common experiences that enrolled college students share. While often highly effective, these programs often end up being perceived as somewhat exclusive in that they are geared toward the students attending that ministry's target campus. As one twenty-seven-year-old said to me, "There's just not a lot in common between me and college students. We're just not at the same point in life."

In addition, there's surprisingly little formal discussion of the challenges to religious faith that this group faces. Ed Stetzer's *Lost and Found: The Younger Unchurched and the Churches that Reach Them* discusses emerging adults from an evangelistic standpoint. David Kinnaman's *UnChristian: What a New Generation of Christians Really Thinks About Christianity* focuses on emerging adults' assessments of how American Christianity is practiced. And *Souls in Transition: The Religious and Spiritual Lives of Emerging Adults* by Christian Smith and Patricia Snell offers an empirically well-grounded snapshot of emerging adults' religious beliefs and practice.

A few books squarely address emerging adults' religious faith. Brett Hoover's *Losing Your Religion, Finding Your Religious Faith* speaks to some of the changes in emerging adults' religious faith. Several books are aimed at college students seeking to assist them in keeping their faith during their college years (e.g. *Own Your Faith: The Adventure of Following Christ in College,* by Mark Tabb). Occasionally someone will write about how religious organizations ought to respond to emerging adults. Tim Muldoon's *Seeds of Hope: Young Adults in the Catholic Church in the United States* and Steve Rabey's *In Search of Authentic Faith: How Emerging Generations are Changing the Church* are examples of these kinds of books. And, there are a few books, such as Jennifer Ruisch's *Faith and the City: A Girl's Search for Post-College Meaning*, that offer a reflection on an emerging adult's personal faith journey.

More importantly, emerging adults themselves feel overlooked. Rightly or wrongly, they perceive that, like the middle of five children, they get lost in the shuffle. One twenty-four-year-old said, "The people at church are great. They're kind and loving; great Christians and all. But they don't know what to do with me. There's not really anything for people my age there. So, I don't go there anymore." Another twenty-two-year-old lamented, "I miss the youth group! I wish there was a youth group for twenty-two-year-olds!" They notice it when there's a youth minister, but not an emerging adult minister. They notice it when families sit together, teenagers sit together, and senior citizens sit together at worship while they sit alone. They notice it when there's not a section of the church bulletin devoted to the activities of that group of people where they are in life. An otherwise self-confident, mature twenty-six-year-old said of the people at her church, "They wouldn't miss me if I were to leave." And, one somewhat cynical twenty-three-year-old responded to my query about being overlooked by observing, "I don't give a lot of money to the church. I don't drive a nice car. I don't have a family. I can't lead worship or anything like that. What do I have to offer them? Of course they're going to overlook me! It is what it is."

The Wilderness

How can we best understand the plight of today's Christian emerging adults? For me, it works best to say that many of them are wandering in the wilderness. The Old Testament tells us that because of their rebelliousness the Israelites were made to wander in the Judean wilderness for forty years before entering the land God promised them. As commonly used, the word "wilderness" refers to a rugged, uncivilized area suggesting danger. However, the word is also an apt description of a time during which a Christian experiences uncertainty, change, and danger. As one emerging adult told me, "I spent my time in the wilderness. It wasn't fun and I regret it." Another remarked, "I wasn't prepared for the changes in my religious faith after I graduated from college. They kicked my butt."

Howard Brinton believes that one of the most significant changes in emerging adults' religious life is that they enter a phase of great uncertainty—about themselves, about what they believe, about how they ought to live, and about where they're headed.[1] He describes this as a time of inner tension and struggle resulting in a divided self and a time of wilderness. Though adolescents experience this to some extent, it explodes into full significance for emerging adults. Indeed, as I reflect on many of the emerging adults I have known over the years, this metaphor seems most apt. It accurately describes their religious journey. As their former teacher, mentor, friend and Christian brother, I have felt great concern as so many of them seem to flounder in their Christian faith. And, I have had it on my heart to do something to speak to their wilderness experience.

For several years I have been the preaching minister for a church of about 450 people. I choose to fill that position because I believe that there are divinely-revealed biblical principles that inform any conversation about faith and life. Thus, I incorporate those ideas into any discussion of emerging adults' religious faith. Yet I am also a college teacher, having taught for over twenty-two years for three different schools. In many ways my life's work has been to educate and influence emerging adults. In anticipation of this project, I have made it a point to candidly discuss matters of religious faith and practice with a large number of my post-college students who were willing to do so. I hope to reflect their experiences and thoughts, using them to better understand how they see the challenges to their religious faith. Finally, I am a social scientist at heart. Trained in graduate school to study and teach communication and religion through a sociological lens, I have come to see the usefulness of looking at human behavior as a social scientist does. Though such a lens can only take us so far in understanding the mysteries of religious faith, I fully believe that academic theories and research are helpful in more fully understanding faith's complexities.

As I survey the scene, what is lacking is a perspective on emerging adults' religious faith that integrates several strands of thought: Biblically based principles, empirical academic research, and real-life first-person accounts. This book seeks to draw together each of these strands so as to address the challenges facing emerging adults' religious faith and offer suggestions for successfully overcoming those challenges. Along the way, the book will speak to what concerned parents and churches ought to know and do to assist emerging adults in navigating the tough terrain they face.

The plastic trays were littered with the wrappers, used napkins, and packets of sauce common to many fast food meals. As my former student rose to make her exit at the end of our hour and a half conversation, she emptied her tray into the nearby trash can, turned to me and said, "You know, Brian, you ought to write a book about faith after college. I'll bet a lot of people would read it." "Sure," I said dismissively. "In all my spare time I'll write that book."

We parted company in the parking lot, and I have not seen her in the eleven years since then. However, not long ago I noticed that on her Facebook page she listed her religion as "Atheist." As I stared at the screen, I knew it was time to write the book.

DISCUSSION QUESTIONS

1. Think about some of the emerging adults that you know. What are their struggles? What are your concerns for them and their Christian faith?

2. If you're old enough, think back to what it was like when you were an emerging adult. What were your experiences? In what ways were they different or similar to emerging adults' experiences today?

3. This chapter claims that emerging adults are a "forgotten group." Do you agree with that assessment? If so, why do you think they are overlooked?

4. What ideas from the Bible do you think might be especially relevant to emerging adults?

5. If you're an emerging adult, what would you want to say to adults about emerging adulthood? If you're an adult, what advice would you give to emerging adults about that time of life?

What Is an Emerging Adult?

"I guess I'm an adult; I'm just not a real adult."

There's often a time when you first awake in the morning when you're no longer asleep and yet not quite awake. Things are unclear and confusing. You're often not sure if you want to wake up or stay asleep. What do you call that time?

There's often a time in the course of a relationship when you're more than friends, but not quite romantically involved with one another. You have feelings for the other person that transcend friendship, but the two of you are definitely not dating; in fact you might not be certain that the other person even reciprocates your changing affection. So, previously smooth interactions sometimes become awkward as you try to subtly but unmistakably ascertain where the relationship is going. What do you call that time?

It's difficult to be in between things. Most of us prefer the comfort of knowing exactly where we stand with respect to things. We prefer to either be wide awake or soundly asleep, for both states are much more pleasant when you're firmly in one or the other. We prefer to know that we are either "just friends" or "a couple," for such designations come with a fairly clear-cut, understandable set of expectations as to how we will interact with one another. But being in between things throws us off. Lacking clear guidelines as to how to think, act, speak, and feel, we struggle. As author Marilyn Ferguson said, "It's not so much that we're afraid of change or so in love with the old ways, but it's that place in between that we fear. It's like being between trapezes. It's Linus when his blanket is in the dryer. There's nothing to hold on to."

Ask any emerging adult and he or she will likely understand exactly what Ferguson means, for they live "in that place in between." Knowing that they are no longer teenagers but not feeling fully grown up yet, they experience life for several years suspended in mid-air between the trapeze of adolescence and the trapeze of adulthood. This was brought home to me a few years ago when I talked with one of my former college students. Largely directionless after graduating from college, she bounced from job to job hoping to find a career path for which she could be enthusiastic. That led her to graduate school and a shared rental house with three other women, each making her own way in the world. Though she was on her own, her parents paid a portion of her monthly rent to help her make ends meet. She wasn't dating anyone, and while she liked graduate school, she often wondered why she was pursuing an advanced degree when she wasn't even sure what she wanted to do for a living. She was clearly not thrilled with where she was in life at that moment, and to lighten the melancholy mood a bit I said something along the lines of, "It's tough to grow up, isn't it? Sometimes being an adult isn't all that it's cracked up to be." She smiled wryly and replied, "I don't really feel like an adult." Then she sighed and said, "I guess I'm an adult. I'm just not a real adult."

A "real adult?" What does that mean? At first glance you might think that by "real adult" she meant that there is authentic and imposter adulthood. However, upon closer inspection it seems to me that what she really meant was complete and incomplete adulthood. Her words give voice to the notion that adulthood is not something into which one abruptly transitions. Instead, adulthood today is an unfolding process, not unlike that of a caterpillar transforming itself into a butterfly. We live in a time when a new phase of the American life cycle has been created; as we shall see, it is the product of postponed transitions to adulthood, the structure of our institutions, and shifts in attitudes toward adulthood.

Adulthood Delayed

When does someone become an adult? Many cultures used to have clear-cut thresholds of adulthood which, once passed, proclaimed to all that you were an adult. For example, in many Native American cultures, boys became adults upon completing a rite-of-passage ritual. In the United States, one legally becomes an adult at age eighteen. Most of us don't just link definitions of adulthood to a specific age but to some other culturally defined set of indicators. I recently asked a random sample of twenty-five people between the ages of eighteen and seventy to answer this question: when does someone become an adult? Three of them said at age eighteen and left it at that, but the other twenty-two offered a variety of responses. Many said, "When you get out on your own." Several said, "When you get married." Yet another said, "When you are financially independent." One even said, "You're not an adult until you have kids of your own!" This small, unscientific sample indicates the diversity of opinions as to when one enters "real adulthood" and brings into clear view a key point: though there are no culturally agreed-upon lines between adulthood and what goes before it, there are a cluster of events which Americans tend to say cumulatively indicate adulthood.

Sociologist Jeffrey Arnett is the foremost scholar studying emerging adults. In his book, *Emerging Adults in America: Coming of Age in the 21st Century*, he describes what have come to be the broadly accepted indicators of adulthood in American society. As in my informal survey, these include completing education, establishing financial independence, getting married, and having children. But Arnett notes that since 1950 there has been a trend in America toward delaying or postponing the things which complete the transformation into full adulthood. As Americans ages twenty to twenty-nine delay their transition to full adulthood, they create another phase of the life cycle: emerging adulthood. Emerging adulthood is not necessarily defined by age, though most agree that Emerging Adults are ages twenty to twenty-nine. Nor is it strictly defined by events, though many believe that the more life milestones one reaches the closer one gets to full adulthood.

For example, marriage has been one of the most commonly accepted indicators of adulthood. Yet evidence now shows that Americans are delaying marriage. The median age at which American women are first married was twenty in 1950 and twenty-five in 2000. For men it was twenty-three in 1950 and twenty-seven in 2000 (men have historically been two years older at the age of first marriage than women).[1] Furthermore, a smaller proportion of emerging adults are married by age thirty. Only 38% of men and 48% of women are married by age thirty yet 68% of both sexes are married by age forty.[2] The fact is, far fewer people are married during their twenties (as opposed to being single, divorced, or living together) than in previous generations. Whereas in the 1970s the vast majority of people in their late twenties were married, that is no longer the case.

Another indication of adulthood is having children, and there too we see a postponement. In 1959, the average age at which American women had their first child was twenty-one. In 2006 it was twenty-five. And, it is more common now than ever before for women to have their first child after age thirty. The birth rate for women in their thirties and forties has doubled since the late 1970s. Finally, the percentage of emerging adults reporting that they live in a home with children of their own has declined from 42% in 1970 to 23% in 2000.[3]

Emerging adulthood has also come about due to the explosion of Americans participating in higher education. The percentage of eighteen to twenty-four year olds attending college has risen from 20% in 1950 to over 60% in 2000. Women in particular have entered higher education in greater proportions. In 1967, only about 20% of women ages eighteen to twenty-four attended college; in 2005 42% did.[4] And today women make up a majority (57%) of the undergraduate students on American college campuses.[5] Such extensive participation in academic pursuits delays marriage, which in turn delays having children, and so the transitions into adult life are further postponed.

Finally, for many Americans "putting down roots" is a marker of adulthood. One aspect of settling down is staying in one place for an extended period of time. Indeed, in the period immediately after World War II most Americans moved out of their parents' home and were not likely to move much after that. However, today emerging adults are more mobile than ever before. Over a third of people between the ages of twenty and twenty-four report that they have moved within the past year, while only 18% of those thirty to thirty-four and 10% of those forty to forty-four have done so.[6] Pursuing higher education and changing locations to follow career paths mean that this marker of adulthood is also postponed.

Of course, part of this is demographics. In 1950, the average American man lived to be sixty-five years old and the average women reached seventy. But in 2010 the average man could expect to live until seventy-five and the average woman could expect to see eighty.[7] People simply live longer today, and so it is logical that lengthened life expectancies might stretch out the distance between life transitions. But demographics alone cannot account for all of this change. Americans are making different choices now than in previous generations, and this is clearly captured in research by sociologist Frank Furstenburg and his colleagues. They examined the percentage of people who had completed all of the major transitional events into adulthood (leaving home, being financially independent, and getting married). In 1960, 77% of American women and 65% of American men had completed all such life transitions by the time they turned thirty. However, in 2000 only 46% of the women and 31% of the men had done so.[8]

On Their Own

In addition to delayed life transitions, another phenomenon also brings about emerging adulthood, and it is conveniently illustrated in most churches. The church I attend has an extensive program for children from the cradle roll through elementary school. There are age-specific classes with a rotation of some of the most caring, invested teachers in our church. For elementary aged kids, there are Christian leadership development opportunities and social activities too. Many churches have paid children's ministers who oversee such programs and some Christian colleges have undergraduate programs training people to fill such positions. Publishing houses create pre-packaged curriculum tailored to their learning level and developmental needs. Likewise, the kids in junior and senior high school are well looked after. My church of four hundred has a paid youth minister crafting a robust program of instruction, social activities, ministry, and worship. A significant amount of time and money is invested in teenagers with the aim of broadening and cementing their Christian faith. Again, there are college degrees to be earned for those who work with teenagers, plus a plethora of books on ministering to adolescents. In short, Christian children, youth, and teenagers get a lot of support and attention. And rightly so, for the Bible reminds us that if we "Train up a child in the way he should go when he is old he will not depart from it" (Proverbs 22:6).

In many ways this is in keeping with the larger society which also offers a significant amount of institutional support. Pre-schools, elementary schools, and junior and senior high schools all function as what some sociologists have called caretaker institutions. These not only educate young people, they also function as powerful agents of socialization helping them learn how to fit neatly into society. Indeed, as one grows up he or she will spend most waking hours interacting with these institutions. And it doesn't stop there, for after high school those who continue on to college encounter another (albeit less controlling) caretaker institution.

However, the extensive institutional support offered from pre-school through college suddenly falls off during the period of emerging adulthood. Maybe we assume that the job is done or that whatever is left to be learned can be accomplished on one's own. Maybe we think they should be grown up by age twenty-two and, if they aren't, well then that's too bad. For whatever reason, our society and our churches simply do not provide the same kind of institutional support for emerging adults as we do younger people. That's why there are far fewer emerging adult ministers than youth or children's ministers. That's why there are fewer books written about developing the emerging adult's faith. That's why at my church there is no formal programming for emerging adults.

Researchers have noted this situation and believe that this sudden drop-off carries significant implications for emerging adults. In the past, the major events transitioning to full adulthood occurred when people were still under the significant influence of key supporting institutions. But now emerging adults effectively push those transitional events to a time when the traditional institutional support has ended. As one scholar concluded, "Younger adults are having to invent their own ways of making decisions and seeking support for those decisions. Whereas dating and mate selection used to happen within the social milieu of the high school, congregation or campus, it now occurs increasingly in bars, at parties, and through the Internet. Other major decisions, such as where to live and what kind of career to pursue, are also being made on an improvisational basis, largely without firm institutional grounding."[9]

For example, I attended a Christian college and, like many of my peers, I met my spouse during my college years. We dated during college and married at age twenty-two, immediately after graduating from college. So our courtship was spent under the influence of a Christian college and the church involvement that came along with it. But that was in 1987. As we have seen, since then the average age at first marriage has risen to twenty-seven. If she and I were to replicate that today, we would marry at twenty-seven, dating a few years prior to that, say, twenty-four to twenty-seven. We would have been in college when we met (who knows how we would've met then!), and our entire courtship would have unfolded apart from any institutional support, except perhaps a church. Would I have still felt it as important to marry a Christian? Would I have met enough women to conclude that there were realistic Christian candidates for marriage? Would she and I have as successfully maintained our sexual purity prior to marriage? Though I want to say "yes" to these questions, I must also admit that the likelihood of the positive outcomes I experienced were increased because of the institutional support I experienced as a young adult. I have no doubt that, at least in my case, delaying my decision to marry would have decreased the likelihood of such positive results.

And that's the point. Emerging adults are more often on their own as they navigate toward full adulthood and therefore at greater risk of being shipwrecked along the way. Furthermore, as a society and as Christians we seem to be tacitly okay with that. Otherwise, we would be channeling a lot more time and effort into emerging adults than we currently do.

"Yes, but not yet"

I admit it. When I was a very young child I used to play house. A few of my cousins would visit and we would pretend that we were "grown ups." One cousin would be the mom, another the dad, and I would always land the role of the teenage son who was a star on the local high school football team. Of course, I outgrew that stage, but the desire to be older than I really was continued. I vividly remember sitting in my homeroom as an elementary school student watching the seemingly mature junior high students remove things from their lockers and thinking, "Wow! I can't wait to get to junior high, travel from classroom to classroom, and have my own locker." Upon entering junior high, I recall seeing high school students who wore letterman's jackets and drove cars. I saw them and thought, "Wow! I can't wait to get into high school and start driving!" As fate would have it, I made it to high school and got my driver's license. However, soon thereafter I saw college students and began dreaming of the time when I could move out of state to attend college and become a real adult. In short, I always wanted to transition to the next stage of life. And the older I got the more I anticipated becoming an adult, that wondrous time of life full of exciting possibilities.

Things have changed a bit since then. Emerging adults see adulthood differently than did previous generations. Two or three generations ago, the goal of Americans was to enter adulthood as quickly as possible, "settle down," and get started in the important business of career and family. The events of adulthood such as marriage and children were seen as achievements and indicated success. But as sociologist Jeffrey Arnett explains,

> The young people of today see adulthood in quite a different light. In their late teens and early twenties, marriage home, and children are seen by most of them not as achievements to be pursued but as perils to be avoided. It is not that they do not want marriage or a home and (one or two) children—eventually. Most of them do want to take on those obligations, and most of them will have done so by the time they reach age 30. It is just that, in their late teens and early twenties, they ponder such obligations and think, "Yes, but not yet." Adulthood and its obligations offer security and stability, but they also represent the closing of doors—the end of independence, the end of spontaneity, the end of a sense of wide-open responsibilities.[10]

"Yes, but not yet." This sort of thinking about adulthood and all that comes with it is only exacerbated by the increasing number of emerging adults who live at home with their parents; 40% of them will move back in with parents. This trend is encouraged by the alarming proportion of the male segment of emerging adults whose leisure activities are spent playing video games: 48% of men ages eighteen to thirty-four play video games an average of 2.5 hours per day. It is celebrated in raunchy movies like *Knocked Up, Old School,* and *40 Year-Old Virgin,* which portray men who are old enough to have embraced full adulthood but forestall it through any means possible. In fact, in his book *Guyland: The Perilous World Where Boys Become Men,* sociologist Michael Kimmel notes that males are especially susceptible to the "Yes, but not yet" thinking.

This sort of thinking seems to deviate from Paul's words in 1 Corinthians 13:11 where he states, "When I became a man I put childish ways behind me." Emerging adults' penchant for prolonging a period in their life of diminished responsibilities is not in itself a bad thing. But it can easily become a stumbling block. For example, attaining many of the life transitions associated with adulthood is often accompanied by greater involvement in church life. "Yes, but not yet" thinking might be extended to church life too, such that involvement and leadership positions are neglected since they represent responsibilities associated with adulthood. This is evident in the comment made to me when I asked an emerging adult to assist with a worship service at the church I attend. He declined my overture for assistance saying that he didn't feel ready for that yet.

When Do You Become an Adult?

Emerging adults also have a different view of when one becomes an adult. Let's return to my former student, mentioned earlier in the chapter. Her words were, in part, "I guess I'm a real adult." *I guess* I'm a real adult? That phrasing suggests that she was uncertain as to whether or not she was an adult, and in doing so she is reflecting the prevailing attitude among her peers. Jeffrey Arnett's research asked thousands of emerging adults, "Do you feel that you have reached adulthood?" Fully 60% of them said "yes and no" in response. However, virtually none in their thirties and forties in Arnett's survey responded that way; nearly all of them answered with a definitive "yes."

This points to a pervasive uncertainty about identity, and when people's identity is uncertain, so are their actions. That's why in 2 Peter 2:9 the author reminds Christians of their identity as "a chosen people, a royal priesthood, a holy nation, a people belonging to God" and encourages them to act in accordance with that identity. One emerging adult explained to me why she wasn't attending church any more. After I had gently but firmly rebutted her excuses, she finally said in frustration, "Look! I'm sure I'll start going to church later on after I've established myself. But I'm just not there yet. So don't worry about me, okay?" But I do worry about her, and to the best of my knowledge she has yet to start attending church.

Yet, it is not as if emerging adults are completely clueless as to when they have reached full adulthood. From his surveys and interviews with thousands of emerging adults, Arnett concludes: "Becoming an adult today means becoming self sufficient, learning to stand alone as an independent person."[11] Since that may strike you as vague, Arnett goes on to explain that emerging adults define being self sufficient as taking responsibility for oneself, making independent decisions, and being financially independent.

Think about what this implies. First, it implies that some of the traditional indicators of adulthood favorable to the Christian faith are no longer associated with adulthood. For example, based on the description in Genesis 2:24 of a man leaving his father and mother and being united to his wife in marriage, Christians have typically associated marriage with adulthood. Yet emerging adults tend to see things differently. Second, it implies that churches cannot simply assume that because emerging adults reach a certain age that they feel comfortable participating in the classes and programs designed for adults.

The Search for the Ideal

Emerging adults think differently in another way as well: they are searching for the ideal version of things. To explain this, consider what a teenager knows of marriage. Most teenagers are not yet married, so their only frame of reference is a marriage which they observe second-hand, whether it be their own parents' marriage, portrayals of marriage in the media, or someone else's marriage. But since marriage is not on most teens' radar, and since they lack the life experience and psychological development required to substantially understand marriage, they have what might be called a *limited* view of marriage. Full adults, on the other hand, have the benefit of both more life experience and greater maturity. Plus, many of them have direct experience with marriage; they have experienced it first-hand, warts and all. Thus, they have what might be called a *realistic* view of marriage. Emerging adults are in between teenagers and adults. Marriage is on their radar; they are mature enough to better understand it. And, while they are certainly aware of some realities of marriage, they are optimistic enough to believe that somehow they can navigate the treacherous marital waters and have a happy marriage. They think, "Yes, there are some challenges, but I can make it work." In short, they hold an *ideal* view of marriage. They often think the same way about other areas of life too. As Arnett said, "Despite the stresses of emerging adulthood, it is for most people a time of high hopes and big dreams. When emerging adults look toward the future, they see fulfillment of their hopes in love and work; a lifelong, harmonious, happy marriage; happy thriving children; and satisfying and lucrative work. In their twenties, it is still possible for emerging adults to believe that everything will work out as they planned, because even if things are going badly now, no doors are firmly closed, few decisions are irrevocable, their dreams may yet prevail."[12] This sense of optimism prevails because emerging adults perceive that they have the freedom and skills to attain the ideal.

Emerging adults apply this sort of optimistic thinking to religion too, though in a slightly different way. By the time they reach emerging adulthood, Christians are old enough to have seen religion's strengths and weaknesses. Their response is often what Sharon Parks calls "Searching for the Ideal." By this she means that emerging adults are seeking what is "pure, consistent, authentic, and congruent."[13] They expect religious faith and practice to live up to its billing. They might assume that if you're a Christian, you'll act like one. They might assume that if prayer is as powerful as it is claimed to be, then it will be effective all of the time. Since emerging adults can now choose their own life commitments, they desire to commit themselves to something that works; if they find it, then they conclude that religion is worthy of their commitment and jump in fully. Yet the yardstick by which they measure religious beliefs is the question, "Is this what religion is supposed to be?" That is, "Does it live up to the ideal?"

One thing many have observed about Christian emerging adults in the early twenty-first century is their affinity for social justice ministries. They look favorably on activities in which Christians are actively putting their faith into action, especially actions that meet the physical needs of the most vulnerable in our society. For example, many emerging adults I know get excited about feeding the homeless, working with Habitat for

Humanity, volunteering at shelters for victims of domestic violence, or raising money to provide potable drinking water in developing nations. They're less interested in teaching Bible classes, visiting people in hospitals, or attending seminars. Why? Because they see the former as more pure or authentic expressions of faith and the latter as less so. Other emerging adults I know are drawn to worship services that are casual in dress, diverse in audience composition, and especially heartfelt in emotional tone. Why? Again because such worship services are perceived to be pure and authentic.

Notice that, at least for those emerging adults raised as Christians, the underlying assumption is that consistent, authentic, and congruent religion exists. It merely has to be found through a search process. Many people simplistically believe that emerging adults have given up on church and religion. That's not the case at all. As we will see in the next chapter, emerging adults' faith and practice is stronger than we often think. However, it is the case that if emerging adults search for the ideal and cannot find it, then they become disillusioned and abandon either church or faith or both. This at least partially explains why many emerging adults switch faith traditions. In fact, in some research, up to 50% of them switch faith traditions.[14]

Good

Four Features of the Twenties

Jeffrey Arnett offers four features of emerging adulthood that make it different from what precedes it (adolescence) and what follows it (young adulthood). Each of Arnett's features carries significant implications for the faith of the twentysomethings.

First, emerging adulthood is a time of identity exploration. As Arnett writes, "Emerging adulthood is the age of identity explorations in the sense that it is the period when people are most likely to be exploring various possibilities for their lives in a variety of areas, especially love and work, as a prelude to making enduring choices that will set the foundation for their adult lives. . . . Emerging adults clarify their identities, that is they learn more about who they are and what they want out of life."[15] Whereas teenagers have only begun to consider such questions, emerging adults, by virtue of their greater maturity and larger bank of life experiences, can do so with greater breadth and depth. These explorations form the backdrop for and extend to emerging adults' Christian life. As one emerging adult said to me, "Right now I'm trying to figure out where I'm going and who I want to be." Another said this about what he is currently doing with his life: "I'm just keeping it real, hanging out looking around to see what I want to be about, you know?"

One way this manifests itself in emerging adults' Christian lives is in their commitment to a particular faith tradition. One of the frustrations I experienced as a Christian college teacher was that during college or upon graduation many of my students would shed their affiliation with the Christian faith tradition in which they were raised. Despite attending a college affiliated with and supportive of the faith tradition of their youth, it was common for them to try out an affiliation with others. I queried one of my former students about this, and she simply replied, "I'm checking out the other options . . . sort of like dating before getting married." Such an attitude irritated and perplexed the student's parents and understandably so. Not only did the parents have a vested interest in seeing their child "stay in the fold," they couldn't understand the notion of exploration because nothing in their own experiences approximated it. There wasn't an "emerging adulthood" when her parents were that age, and so they have no frame of reference. This helps explain the tension that's sometimes felt between emerging adults and their parents.

Second, emerging adulthood is a time of instability. Emerging adults are frequently on the move. Many leave home to go to college; others simply move out. Of those who go to a residential college, many live on campus for a few years and then find housing off campus. About 40% of emerging adults move back in with their parents again for an extended period of time at some point before age thirty.[16] In addition, a high proportion of them move in with a member of the opposite sex. Others move across the country to follow jobs or relationships. As Arnett observes, "Residential changes in the United States peak during Emerging Adulthood."[17]

This instability means that emerging adults are frequently cut off from established relationships, especially established Christian friendships and church affiliations. While ideally they would replace such relationships with others in their new place of residence, there is no guarantee that emerging adults will do so. In fact, anecdotal evidence suggests that emerging adults struggle mightily with this. One of them explained that, "Moving to a new city was one of the hardest things I had ever done. I didn't know anyone; I didn't have any friends and I didn't know where to go to church." When asked how she responded to this unsettling situation, she replied, "I made a few friends at work—none of whom were Christians. I never did find a church; truthfully, I didn't try that hard. It was just as well because I ended up moving again in six months anyway."

I have heard many parents of emerging adult children remark that significant changes in their children's faith coincided with changes in their children's living situation. In the midst of relating how their daughter drifted away from her Christian faith, one couple told me, "Our daughter was okay when she left home and all through college. But things started to change when she moved from the South to the Pacific Northwest. She did so to be closer to her boyfriend and pretty soon they moved in together. Of course, we were opposed to that, but what could we do? So, then it was just her and him because she didn't know anybody else and she certainly wasn't interested in going to church."

(3) Third, emerging adulthood, according to Arnett, is a time of rampant self-focus. He explains, "Emerging adults are self-focused in the sense that they have little in the way of social obligations, little in the way of duties, little in the way of commitments to others, which leaves them a great deal of autonomy in running their own lives. . . . The self-focused quality of emerging adulthood makes it arguably the freest time of their life."[18] It's not that emerging adults are necessarily selfish or self-absorbed; they're simply in a season of life when they are not as "tied down by things." Since for most of them marriage comes closer to age thirty than age twenty and since many of them will switch jobs with great frequency during the same period, they are

unencumbered in ways they will not be in their thirties. While it provides valuable opportunities to engage in the process of exploration mentioned above, it also offers great temptation to waste time and miss opportunities. Looking back on his twenties, one of my former students said, "I wasted so much time during and right after college. I was young and single with nothing to tie me down. I played a lot of video games and spent way too much time online. Way, way too much time! But, I guess it was good to get it out of my system then because you sure can't do that sort of thing once you're married."

This self-focus often precludes the sort of ties that motivate participation in church life. Without a spouse to encourage church involvement, attendance easily wanes. Without children who need the religious and moral instruction that churches offer, there's less reason to make church life a priority. Many emerging adults were accustomed to the accountability provided by parents, friends, and church family, and when they find themselves free from those watchful eyes, they slip in their Christian life. And it seems that few churches make significant, intentional efforts to integrate the Twenties into their programs and ministries. So, many emerging adults don't feel needed at church and thus lack an additional reason to get involved in church life.

Finally, emerging adulthood is an age of possibilities. By this Arnett means two things. First, it is a period of life that generally features great optimism. Arnett explains that, "In Emerging Adulthood, virtually no one expects to end up with a dreary, dead-end job or join the nearly 50% of Americans whose marriages end in divorce, or make mistakes that drive life into a ditch. Even if their current lives are a struggle, as is the case for many emerging adults, they continue to believe that they will ultimately prevail. During emerging adulthood, hopes reign."[19] In Romans 10:2, Paul writes about those who have zeal but lack knowledge. Emerging adults certainly have zeal for life, but their knowledge is limited by a lack of life experience. Nonetheless, their optimism remains. I have seen this repeatedly in the college students who stand on the precipice of graduation. At age twenty-two, twenty-three, or twenty-four things seem so clear and attainable to them.

One of my students was set to graduate within the month. When I asked her where she saw her life headed in the next several years, she excitedly outlined a life in which she graduated from college, was hired by a non-profit organization involved in social justice issues, found a loft apartment in the trendiest part of the urban downtown, worked from nine to five, and did volunteer work every weekend. After a few years she wanted to find someone special and then get married, having children "not right away, but definitely before I'm thirty." She said this to me in the midst of the worst economic downturn in seventy-five years and despite the fact that she had no relevant experience or training in any of those endeavors (including romantic relationships!).

The second dimension to emerging adulthood as an age of possibilities is best summed up in the phrase, "A chance to start over." Since children and adolescents have little say in so many matters that directly affect them, they are at the mercy of the choices others make. Therefore, many emerging adults have experienced highly dysfunctional families, grown up in unhealthy churches, borne the brunt of adult alcoholism and infidelity, and weathered multiple household moves. In both physical and metaphorical ways, they were trapped. Yet things change as one enters emerging adulthood. As Arnett explains, "Emerging adulthood is the age of possibilities in part because it represents a chance for young people to transform their lives, to free themselves from an unhealthy family environment, and to turn their lives in a new and better direction."[20]

This is not to say that every emerging adult comes from such a disastrous environment. Fortunately most do not. Still, those who do and those who don't both have the opportunity to use the freedom found in emerging adulthood to craft a new and different life path. This was clearly evident in the life of one of my former students whose teenage years featured his parents' divorce, a single-parent home, a life just above the poverty line, and a co-dependent mother. During his college years, he was able to chart a different, healthier course for his life such that after graduation he secured a good job, developed a robust Christian faith, and nurtured sound relationships.

As he said to me on many occasions during his college years, "I don't want to end up like my mom. This is my chance to be different. I can't blow it."

The notion of possibilities is one of the most clearly positive dynamics influencing the faith of emerging adults. The optimism that infuses it often spills over into their religious life. This partially explains why so many emerging adults choose to become missionaries. In fact, more people head to the mission field during emerging adulthood than any other time of life. It also explains why so many emerging adults are involved in hands-on ministries that others shy away from. I have observed, for example, that emerging adults are more comfortable working in ministries to the homeless, street people, prostitutes, and the urban poor than any other age group. They genuinely believe it is possible for them to make a difference.

Epilogue

The student whose story began this chapter didn't feel like a "real adult." We parted company after our meeting and I have not seen her since; as I write this book, it has been over six years. I would like to tell you that she eventually "felt like an adult" and that coming to that revelation opened her eyes to many things. I would like to tell you that her faith is strong, that she's a vibrant member of a church family, and that she is "living a life worthy of the calling that you have received" (Ephesians 4:1). But I can't. The truth is, I don't know what happened to her.

I share this to emphasize that we all know someone like that—an emerging adult suspended in mid-air between the trapeze of adolescence and that of adulthood. Jesus reminds us in Luke 15:1-4 that sometimes sheep get lost. Emerging adulthood is a time of life when sheep, in their confusion and uncertainty, are prone to wander off and get lost. Pray that we may retrieve them and bring them back home.

DISCUSSION QUESTIONS

1. To what extent do you think emerging adulthood is truly a new and unique phase of life?

2. Have you seen evidence of Sharon Parks' "Search for the Ideal"? Is such an attitude helpful or harmful?

3. Consider Jeffrey Arnett's Four Features of Emerging Adulthood. In what ways have you seen emerging adults exemplify these features?

4. In what ways might Arnett's four features of emerging adulthood be a positive or negative influence on Christian faith?

5. Are there any scriptures or biblical principles which might help understand emerging adulthood?

2

Changes in Emerging Adults' Christian Faith

"I guess I just see things differently now."

T he silence after those words stretched a long time. I was walking with one of my former students through a quiet neighborhood not far from the college campus where I taught. Though the sun was bright and the brilliant colors of autumn in the Pacific Northwest were in full blaze, my mood certainly didn't match the scene around me. Walking beside me was a twenty-six-year old whom I had known for eight years since she came to my campus, earned a degree, and was now making her way in life. Only she wasn't making her way in life. Four years out of college she was direction-less, struggling in every area of her life. She had not found a career that did anything for her other than pay the bills. She wanted to be married, but couldn't find a guy worthy of her. To make things worse, many of her friends had married in the past few years and she was feeling increasingly alone. Her parents wanted her to return to her hometown to be near family, but she was determined to prove her independence by staying in Portland, Oregon, several hours distant.

All of that was discouraging enough, but the bad news reached a crescendo when the conversation turned to her Christian faith. I had asked her about her faith: where she was attending church, the status of her faith, whether she still prayed, and how close she felt to God. Her first reply was to scoff, saying of her faith, "It's dormant." Then she quickly corrected herself and added, "No, that's not true. It's changed." As the fallen leaves crunched beneath our feet on the sidewalk, she told me that she didn't attend church much anymore and when she did it wasn't a church affiliated with the faith tradition in which she was raised. She spoke of frustration with "organized religion" and disappointment with Christian hypocrisy. With a mixture of regret and liberation in her voice, she explained how she had shed many of the doctrinal beliefs about salvation and Christian practice taught to her as a child. As the afternoon shadows of late October grew longer, she summed it up by saying, "I guess I just see things differently now."

Emerging adulthood is a time of significant changes in a person's Christian life. In fact, though we often believe that adolescence is the crucial period in the formation of a person's Christian faith, the truth is that emerging adulthood may be more so. Understanding emerging adults requires grasping how Christian faith changes as one ages, and fortunately a large body of social scientific study helps us chart this process. Knowing how the process works in the big picture provides a valuable window into emerging adults' Christian faith and practice.

Of course, it certainly comes as no surprise to say that as you grow older your Christian faith changes. As they look back on their lives, most Christians can readily see changes, whether it be growth or decay. The changes in my own Christian faith have been significant, but one change illustrates the salient points in this chapter. From the time I was in grade school until somewhere in the middle of college, I used to believe categorically that the earth was created over a period of six literal, twenty-four-hour days. For me, there was no other possible explanation for creation that was consistent with scripture. But in college I encountered sincere, learned Christians who believed otherwise and I read first-rate, biblically-based material suggesting that there were other means by which God could have created the universe. After these encounters, I gravitated to the position which I now hold: while God *may* have created the universe over the course of six, literal, twenty-four-hour days, *God may have done so in a different manner.* Notice that I'm not questioning the belief that God created the world; I'm merely open to the possibility that God did so in a manner other than the one in which I originally believed. My faith has matured to the point where I can say, "God may have done it this way or that way, but what is most important is that God created the universe. And, my faith is strong enough to bear the ambiguity associated with that." You may sincerely hold a different view on this question, but do not let it obscure the point I am trying to make: some aspects of a person's Christian faith change as he or she gets older.

This process of changing Christian belief is one studied intently by various scholars. Binding the different research projects together is the underlying belief that a person's religious faith develops in the same manner as a human being develops physically, mentally, emotionally, and socially. It is now a rather universally accepted view that clearly marked stages in the development of religious faith correspond to one's age or place in life. These stages provide a powerful insight into a person's religious life as they offer an explanation for observed behavior and suggest ways that people can be shepherded through each stage of the process. Though several scholars have suggested their own scheme detailing these stages, it is beyond the scope of this book to present a thorough discussion of each. Instead, I will mention a few, emphasizing the stage(s) most relevant to emerging adults.

The Need to Choose for Oneself

I grew up in a home where whole milk was served. I put it on my cereal every morning throughout my childhood. It seemed natural and I never questioned it. In fact, I didn't even realize there were other options. Then I went off to college and on my first morning in the campus cafeteria I encountered a milk dispenser with three types of milk. This was unheard of! Despite the presence of 2% and skim milk, I continued exclusively using whole milk. Then I married a woman who drank 2% milk. Though that struck me as odd, I soon tried it and discovered that I liked it better than whole milk. Later on, I converted to 2%, and from there took the plunge and became a devoted skim milk drinker (a commitment I retain to this day).

Why this little story about milk? My milk experience is not unlike what emerging adults experience in their religious life. One of the most significant changes they encounter is the realization that they get to (and have to) choose for themselves what they believe. In his book *Adulthood*, psychologist Erik Erickson offers a detailed model describing how people develop and change over time. He explains that one of emerging adults' key concerns is settling on their identity, that is, who they want to be. Obviously one's religious beliefs are a chief component of identity, and so emerging adults address those dimensions too. What Erickson underscores is that for the first time emerging adults now get to craft their own identity; they get to choose for themselves who they want to be. Unlike their pre-teen and teenage years, they experience relatively unencumbered opportunities for real freedom of choice in making significant life decisions and commitments. Erickson calls this fidelity, "the ability to sustain loyalty freely pledged in spite of inevitable contradictions and confusions of value systems."[1] Though not writing from a Christian perspective, Erickson's description of fidelity seems closely related to Christian faith. For example, the description of faith in Hebrews 11:1 as "being sure of what we hope for and certain of what we do not see" fits into Erickson's fidelity.

The idea that religious beliefs are *chosen* rather than inherited means that emerging adults must devise some way of choosing between competing beliefs. Many emerging adults were raised, for example, with the belief that the Bible condemns homosexuality. However, as they move through the life cycle they encounter alternative beliefs challenging that notion. How is one to sort through the competing beliefs? By what criteria are some beliefs accepted and others rejected? Previously, the right answer was whatever emerging adults were taught by some authority figure such as parents, ministers, or the Bible. But now they realize that they are at the point where they get to (and must) choose to retain those beliefs. Even granting the Bible as an authority on the topic is itself a religious belief to be chosen. The enormity and complexity of such choices about belief can be overwhelming. As one emerging adult told me over lunch one day, "Right now I feel as if everything is up for grabs in my faith. I'm not sure what I believe or even how to sort it all out."

Let's not forget that all of this choosing takes place in the midst of many other decisions which must be made about non-religious matters. Emerging adults face a cascade of decisions regarding career, place of residence, selection of friends, the management of money, the pursuit of romantic relationships, to name just a few. Such considerations can be overwhelming for them. As one said, "After I graduated [from college], I was on my own, making my own decisions and living my own life. I wasn't prepared for all of that. After my roommate and I moved our stuff into the apartment, Sunday came and I didn't get up to go to church. My roommate noticed this and asked me about it. She said, 'Isn't church important to you?' I said, 'Yes it is,' but then wondered, 'Is it really?'" If you read carefully between the lines of that comment you'll see that my former student faced a dawning realization that a previously held belief (the importance of church attendance) was unmoored and now open to possible rejection. She had to *choose* to maintain that belief; it didn't just continue on by some process of inertia. This is a significant change, for during their childhood and teenage years emerging adults didn't have to choose what they believed. They just believed because that's what they had always done. Plus, many developmental psychologists hold that even though they "believed" back then they didn't truly believe in the fullest and most mature sense of the word. In other words, they "chose" and "believed" as much as they were able to at the time given their rather limited social, emotional, and intellectual abilities.

Thus far, I have described emerging adults' decisions regarding religious matters as making choices. However, perhaps a better way to understand what they are actually doing is to see them as making commitments. A choice implies a simple selection between alternatives, as when I say that I have chosen to eat at Taco Bell instead of McDonald's. Because I am merely choosing between two fast-food establishments there isn't an expected obligation to make the same choice the next time. But choosing a religious belief is not at all like choosing a fast-food restaurant. Religious beliefs carry far greater significance in our lives and hence they are accompanied by a type of obligation to maintain them. This means that such commitments ought to be made more thoughtfully and adhered to more stringently.

When emerging adults make commitments regarding their religious beliefs, what kinds of commitments do they make? Harvard Psychologist William Perry studied how people move through stages as they come to understand their beliefs. As children, they experience *dualism*, believing that something is right or wrong only because an authority figure tells them so. During the teenage years they move on to *relativism*, where they recognize that multiple answers are possible, and then, as adults, to the *commitment* stage where they commit to one choice from among the multiple answers.[2] As applied to our creation example mentioned previously, I reflected *dualism* when as a child I believed in a literal twenty-four-hour creation timeline because my Bible class teachers taught me that and, by implication, that all other answers were wrong. Later, I reflected *relativism* when I realized that there are other, viable alternatives to that view. Finally, I reflected *commitment* when arriving at my current view, that the world was probably created in seven, literal twenty-four-hour days but that it could have worked out differently.

Sociologist Sharon Parks believes that emerging adults exhibit a stage in between Perry's relativism and commitment, a stage she calls *probing commitment*.[3] In probing commitment someone tentatively commits to something; he or she tries on a belief to see if it fits. The belief is probed or road-tested to see how well it works. There's a more significant investment in the belief than in the relativism stage but not as significant an investment as in the commitment stage. It's a bit like buying a mattress. In my town, several mattress stores offer a thirty-day trial whereby they remove your old mattress, install the new one, and allow you to sleep on it for thirty nights. If you're not happy with it, you can bring it back for a full refund. Of course, it's a rather involved process to get the new mattress into your home, let alone remove it after thirty nights, retrieve your old mattress, and set everything back up again. Parks claims that emerging adulthood is a time of life when people make *probing commitments* to religious beliefs, trying on some beliefs, discarding some, and keeping others.

One of my former students recounted how he had been raised with the belief that the New Testament phenomenon of speaking in tongues no longer existed, and that whatever was claimed to be speaking in tongues was at best misunderstood or at worst fraudulent. Upon graduating from college, he was looking for a church with which to worship, and he happened to try one where speaking in tongues was regularly practiced. Though he felt it odd at first, he continued to attend there, all the while pondering what he believed about speaking in tongues (and even trying it out for himself!). After about six months, he concluded that his original belief on that matter was accurate.

Now, whatever else is going on in his story, my former student had clearly made a probing commitment to a belief in the veracity of speaking in tongues. However, he later rescinded that belief. Parks says that we ought not to be surprised when emerging adults make probing commitments; doing so is natural and to be expected.

Seeing Religious Faith Differently (or "God Said It. I'll Evaluate It.")

One of the most striking changes in emerging adults' understanding of religious faith concerns the notion of authority. Returning to Sharon Parks again, she points out that as one learns about religious faith one also learns that there are proper and improper sources of authority, insight, and truth. During childhood and adolescence, we are taught that religious authority rests in sources outside of ourselves—in parents, the Bible, teachers, and ministers. This deference to authority is reflected in the songs that children sing ("Jesus loves me, this I know, for the Bible tells me so.") and the bumper stickers that adults put on their cars ("God said it. I believe it. That settles it."). It is reflected in the fact that people often precede their questions to me with, "You're a minister, so you'll likely know the answer to this." Indeed, the starting point for all religious faith seems to be accepting that someone (God) or something (the Bible) outside oneself has authority. Otherwise, isn't there chaos?

However, Parks notes that emerging adults experience a shift such so that they come to feel that religious authority is located inside themselves as they "recognize that we must take responsibility for one's own knowing, one's own choices—even at the level of religious faith."[4] She characterizes this as moving from a dependence on trusted others to an inner-dependence where one trusts oneself. Emerging adults essentially revise the bumper sticker to read, "God said it. I will evaluate it. Maybe I will believe it." To them, it makes sense to cast themselves in the role of arbiter of what is right or wrong when it comes to religious beliefs. They fully believe that they have the ability and the right to determine for themselves which religious beliefs they will accept or reject.

Notice how the difference in these two ways of seeing religious faith shapes the portion of a discussion of homosexuality between a parent and her daughter, as recounted by one of my former colleagues:

Fifty-five-year old parent: How can you say that homosexuality isn't wrong? The Bible is quite clear on this issue. There are several passages of scripture that make it obvious that homosexuality is a sin. And, there's a long history within the church condemning homosexuality.

Twenty-five-year old child: Yes, but I just don't think God would condemn two people for loving one another. They're not hurting anyone! Why can't we just leave them alone? It doesn't make any sense to say that God is love and that we ought to love one another and then to turn around and say, "Oh, that's only for heterosexuals." I think it threatens us like inter-racial marriage used to and so we try to condemn it on flimsy grounds.

Notice that the fifty-five-year old parent grounds her attack on homosexuality on "outside" authorities such as God, the Bible, and the church. The emerging adult child grounds her defense of homosexuality on "inside" authorities such as whether things make sense to her.

One of the chief criteria by which emerging adults measure religious beliefs is quite simple: "If it works for me, then I'll accept it. If not, then I'll reject it." This sense of pragmatism becomes the litmus test for many religious beliefs. One of my former students was raised in a highly conservative faith tradition that taught a very limited role for women in public worship. As an emerging adult, she reconsidered her belief on that topic and ultimately abandoned it. When asked how this came to be, she explained that her original belief "Just didn't seem right." She went on to say that it "made no sense" to her that God would exclude half the world's population from a role in public worship simply based on gender. Besides, she added, as a woman she felt that she had significant contributions to make to public worship and any belief that precluded her participation is therefore inherently deficient. She is not alone. I know many emerging adults who discern their Christian beliefs in an identical manner. Of course, many will recognize such thinking as akin to postmodern thinking, and this is exactly what it is. But let's not get into all of that; instead, let's simply note that this has significant ramifications for Christian faith.

Surely the bedrock of the Christian faith is that the Bible is the divinely inspired revelation of God and that in it rests all authority and truth. When emerging adults (or anyone else, for that matter) hold themselves up as interpreters of biblical teaching using their own sense of "what's right," all hopes of uniformity of belief are dashed. This scenario reduces Christianity to individual preference based on "whatever works for you." The Ten Commandments become the Ten Suggestions. "I tell you the truth" becomes "I offer this for your consideration." False teachers become alternative viewpoints. To the extent that emerging adults adopt this lens through which to see Christian beliefs they risk an inaccurate or warped understanding of central Christian beliefs.

The Reordered Faith

Thus far, we have seen that emerging adults naturally see their religious faith differently than do those at other points in life. Recognizing the need to choose for themselves and experiencing changes in how they view religious authority result in emerging adults taking on a significant project: remodeling their house of faith. V. Bailey Gillespie's book *Experience of Faith* offers one particularly helpful way of understanding how emerging adults revise their faith. Like others we have discussed, Gillespie conceives of religious faith as developing in stages over a period of time. Gillespie calls the stage of faith development through which people in their twenties move "reordered faith," a time of "restructuring, relearning the life of faith, retesting and sorting out feelings of religion."[5] As Gillespie observes, "Choices have begun to be clarified, directions now are beginning to be known. Career, marriage, job, faith, God's will, all begin to happen together. A certain stability of belief is sought after. A testing of the reality of belief in God occurs now."[6]

The notion of testing religious beliefs is especially important. While in previous stages of life it might have been fine to discuss matters of faith at church, emerging adults have a need to try them out in the real world. In turn, this means that they will often experiment with their beliefs, modifying, assessing, and weighing them to determine their fitness. One emerging adult described to me a period of time during his college years when he stopped attending church. When asked why he did so, his reply was succinct: "I wanted to see what would happen." Having been raised all his life with the belief that attending church was a central part of Christian life, he simply wanted to see if that were true when submitted to a real-world test. Since he was living under his parent's roof during his childhood and adolescence, he had no opportunity to test that belief. Moving to another state to attend college afforded him the chance to do so.

This testing is an important aspect of reordered faith because it allows emerging adults to know for themselves whether the beliefs to which they've assented are strong enough to pass the test (and thus are worthy of maintaining) or whether they will crumble in the face of assay (and thus are better discarded). It's as if they are putting into practice the Psalmist's encouragement to "Taste and see that the LORD is good" (Psalm 34:8). Another emerging adult I know told me how she had been raised to believe that consuming any alcoholic beverage at all was a sin. She strongly adhered to this belief through her high school and college years and, in fact, did not drink. However, after college she found herself in a new city where she knew no one and her core circle of friends became those with whom she worked—and they drank. Soon she too began to drink with them after work or at social functions, and, as she said, "The sky didn't fall." She continued, "I didn't go overboard with it or anything. But I did drink. Frequently. At first I felt really weird about it; I mean I had been raised that drinking was wrong. But then I thought, 'Hey! It's no big deal.' And then I began to wonder what else I had been taught that might not be 100% true."

No More Training Wheels

"I am not a morning person." That's what a freshman college student told me as she explained why she habitually missed her morning class with me. She continued: "Plus, I'm having a hard time getting used to waking myself up every morning. You see, all the time I lived at home my mom woke me up for school each morning. Now that I'm here at college, there's no one to wake me up, so I have to set my own alarm." I did my best not to laugh and casually said, "Welcome to the adult world."

That conversation aptly illustrates another change in emerging adults' Christian faith; namely, that for the first time in their lives they are entirely responsible for their own spiritual growth. Prior to coming to college, that freshman didn't have to expend a lot of effort to wake up in the morning because her mother did it for her. Likewise, teenagers raised in Christian homes don't have to expend much effort to grow spiritually. Their parents typically require or expect them to attend church. They frequently attend churches with substantial youth programs so that all the teen has to do is show up (which is easy when their parents expect them to do so and they want to interact with their peers anyway). But then, teenagers transition into emerging adulthood and everything changes. No one is around to wake them up for church services. There's no attractive program of activities just for them. There's no valued peer group to get plugged into at church. There's not a Bible class just for their age group, so if they study the Bible it has to be on their own.

I used to tell all of the incoming students at the Christian college where I taught, "You're on your own now. Up to this point many of you have been riding the bike of Christian faith with training wheels on; all you had to do was peddle and steer. Now you are responsible for peddling, steering, and the most difficult part—balancing. Plus, with the training wheels on you couldn't fall. Now, without those training wheels, not only can you fall, you can get seriously hurt. So I ask you, do you *really* know how to ride the bike of Christian faith? Are you prepared for what happens when the training wheels come off?" My experience has been that very few emerging adults are prepared for the removal of their faith training wheels. Many have a hard time getting up for church. Most don't have it in them to muster the courage to enter a church with which they are not familiar. Others are uncertain how to select a Bible class to attend if there's no clear-cut class for their age group. The vast majority of them seem to struggle with carving out time to engage in personal prayer or study. A chunk of them lack the courage and initiative to join churches or ministries.

Why do emerging adults struggle with all of this? Some are quick to blame parents, claiming that if the parents had done their job well then they wouldn't be this way. Others place the blame on churches for creating in emerging adults an unhealthy dependence on institutional structures such as youth groups and youth ministers. Others blame emerging adults themselves, saying that they simply need to grow up and do what adults do—ride the bike of faith without training wheels. It seems to me that there's some truth in each of these charges. However, it also seems to me that there is perhaps one other dynamic at work here too. Sociologist Gordon Allport draws a distinction between people who are *extrinsically* religious and people who are *intrinsically* religious. The extrinsically religious demonstrate all of the outward indications of a religious faith, but lack the genuine, authentic commitment to religious life and faith. In essence, they are the ones Jesus had in mind in Matthew 15:8 when he drew on the prophet Isaiah's words to say, "These people honor me with their lips, but their hearts are far from me." In contrast, the intrinsically religious not only demonstrate easily seen manifestations of their religious faith, but also possess deep, authentic, abiding commitments to their faith. In essence, they are the ones who "love the Lord with all their heart, soul, mind, and strength" and "love their neighbor as themselves" (Matthew 22:35-37); they are the ones who will "take up their cross" and follow Jesus (Matthew 16:24). Perhaps emerging adults struggle when the training wheels of faith come off because all those wheels have done is help them to become extrinsically religious. If that's the case, then it raises several troubling questions, such as why we settle for that, whether that merely reflects the parent's faith, and whether that merely reflects what churches are equipped to offer.

Are These Changes Good or Bad?

Choosing for yourself. The end of the training wheels. Shifts in authority. Reordered faith. With so many changes going on in how emerging adults see religious faith it's fair to ask if all of this is good or bad for someone's faith. While ultimately the answer is that it depends on the person, there is every reason to believe that these changes can and regularly do lead to stronger faith. Several emerging adults with whom I spoke pointed to the self-testing of their faith as the crucible in which their faith was forged. Looking back, one who is now in her late twenties said, "When I went off to college, I only believed what my parents taught me. I never really chose it for myself. But in college I was confronted with a lot of things that made me think. I asked hard questions. I branched out and tried on some different beliefs. Some fit,

while others didn't. I don't think I would be here [as a Christian] today if I
hadn't done that." Another noted, "My faith changed a lot during my college years. Some for the bad; but mostly for the good. I know one thing for
sure: I wouldn't trade it. I learned a lot about myself. About who I am and
what I want to believe." And another stated, "I think that everyone has to go
through a time in their life when they question things and work things out for
themselves. If you don't you're not being real." Finally, a long-serving minister added, "They [emerging adults] have to go through a period where they
choose to believe things for themselves. How will they ever know if they chose
it or if they simply parroted back what mom and dad told them? In fact, it's
been my experience that the ones who never choose for themselves are worse
off than those who go through some hard times as they figure things out."

The Bible itself often links testing with religious faith. In Ecclesiastes 2,
the Preacher embarks on the project of determining whether various pleasures are meaningful or meaningless. He then describes how he experienced
such pleasures as a sort of test, which was evidently effective for he properly
concluded that such pleasures are meaningless (Ecclesiastes 2:1). Though
hopefully not indulging to the same extent as the Preacher in Ecclesiastes, it
is fair to say that emerging adults' testing of their beliefs is not substantially
different from the Preacher's. Also, in 2 Corinthians 13:5 Paul encourages
the Corinthians to "Examine yourselves to see whether you are in the faith;
test yourselves." This is precisely what emerging adults do as they pursue a
reordered faith. And, in 1 Thessalonians 5:21 Paul writes, "Test everything.
Hold on to the good." Ironically, the twenties may be doing just that and yet
meeting much resistance for doing so. Taken together, it seems that though
the work of reordering faith creates anxiety and peril it is necessary. While
later chapters will say more about responding to emerging adults' testing
of their Christian faith, the point here is that some testing of beliefs during
this time of life is natural and to be expected. While it bears close watching, it does not necessarily mean that emerging adults are losing their faith.

Still, the fact remains that changes in how emerging adults see their
religious faith can be detrimental too. There certainly is a slippery slope

toward apostasy (Hebrews 2:1). As I mentioned in my book, *Falling Away: Why Christians Lose Their Faith and What Can Be Done About It*, research repeatedly shows that ages eighteen to thirty are at the greatest risk of falling away from their faith, and that most of the twenties who abandon their faith "drift away."[7] Many studies conclude that the twenties are twice as likely to fall away as those in their forties or fifties.[8] This is starkly seen in this comment from one of the twenties: "When I went to college I had a faith. When I left college, my faith was eroding. Three years out of college, my faith is dead." We owe it to emerging adults to prevent others from suffering the same fate.

Epilogue

While checking my e-mail not long ago, a message popped up from the former student with whom I had walked on that bright autumn day. It had been a few years since our leaf-crunching conversation and I had intermittently wondered how she was doing. However, the pace of life prevented me from tracking her down to ask. With great interest I opened her e-mail and immediately noticed the first line: "My faith is alive again." The message went on to describe how she found her way to a loving, supportive church where she found friendship and a niche. She thanked me for my concern and made vague offers to get together next time she was in town. I love a story with a happy ending, don't you? I wish they all ended that way. . . .

Discussion Questions

1. In what ways have you seen emerging adults make what Sharon Parks calls "probing commitments"?

2. How can one helpfully respond to emerging adults' perspective on religious authority?

3. How have you seen emerging adults engage in V. Bailey Gillespie's "re-ordered faith"?

4. How can emerging adults best be equipped to deal with the changes they are likely to experience in their Christian faith?

5. Research finds that emerging adults are at great risk of falling away from their Christian faith. Why is this? What can be done about it?

Emerging Adults' Unique Way of Looking at Christian Faith

If you were to visit the church that I attend and worship with us on a Sunday morning, you would notice that the first two rows are populated by several lovely widows. Every Sunday morning they are there, eager to worship. Had you dropped in an hour earlier, you would have seen them there for Bible class too, while down the hall parents were wrangling their small children to classes of their own. If you were to visit on Wednesday night for our mid-week Bible study, you would surely notice that there are lots of retired folks settling in for the study, plus several families and a smattering of teenagers. But don't expect to see very many emerging adults.

Later on, you might decide to join some of our benevolence groups as they deliver food, furniture, rent money, and other necessities to needy people in our community. You might volunteer to staff one of our three children's programs offered during worship on Sunday mornings. You might help stuff envelopes as part of a mass mailing to supporters of a world-wide mission effort using English lessons. You might even want to help out with our vacation Bible school program for kids in the summer, travel to a small town with several other families from church to put on a children's program for kids there, or answer the call to help a single mom from the church move her belongings to a new apartment across town. But don't expect to see any emerging adults serving alongside you.

Now, you might think that I make those observations to bash emerging adults, criticizing them for their lack of involvement at church. That's not the case at all. I offer those observations to make the point that emerging adults seem to enact their Christian faith differently than do those older and younger than them. Whereas the previous chapter discussed the ways in which emerging adults' Christian faith changes, this chapter explores what emerging adults actually believe when it comes to matters of religion. It examines what they actually do as they live out their faith, how that's different from what they did in their teenage years, and what they will likely do later in life. This is necessary because academic research and my own experiences lead to several uncomfortable conclusions: Emerging adults see their faith differently than do others. They also enact their faith differently. And, they face a different set of challenges to their faith. Therefore, this chapter outlines several of these differences, contrasting the Twenties' faith with their faith prior to and after that phase of life.

Tinkering

Someday, when my parents are both dead, I will inherit their home. I will get all of it, the driveway, the living room, the pool, the yard, the kitchen and all that's in it. I like my parents' home. In fact, I grew up in that home and have fond memories of it. But I already know what I am going to do with the house when I take possession of it. First, I'm going to add a hot tub. Then, I am going to remove several of the shrubs in the backyard. The windows in the master bedroom would look better with blinds than the curtains that currently hang there. The basketball backboard in the driveway also needs to be replaced. Yes, there are several changes I have planned for that old house because it will be my house then, and I will insure that it fits my desires. It will essentially remain the same house; it will just have a few renovations.

What has this got to do with emerging adults' Christian faith? Consider that Christian parents talk about "passing on their faith" to their children.

Thus, it seems that we conceive of faith as if it is like my parents' home: Something to be transferred *in its entirety* from one generation to another. Though they might not always admit it, the underlying assumption is that the parents' Christian faith is complete, having stood the test of time and been refined by life experience. Offspring are expected to accept it as it is, complete and whole. After all, why wouldn't they? It's worked for the parents (and by implication for generations prior) and it ought to work for their children too.

Of course the reality is quite different. The truth is that The Twenties who do assent to the religious faith passed on to them rarely accept that faith with 100% fidelity. In his book, *After the Baby Boomers: How Twenty- and Thirty-Somethings are Shaping the Future of American Religion*, sociologist Robert Wuthnow claims that, when it comes to religion, emerging adults are tinkerers. They take something given to them as whole and tinker with it, adding some things and removing others all the while experimenting to see what works for them and what doesn't. Wuthnow writes: "Like the farmer rummaging through the junk pile for makeshift parts, the spiritual tinkerer is able to shift from a veritable scrap heap of ideas and practices from childhood, from religious organizations, classes, conversations with friends, books, magazines, television programs, and Web sites."[1]

Tinkering comes naturally for emerging adults. Wuthnow explains that you cannot tinker much with your Christian faith in your teenage years because you're constrained by your parents and other elements of institutional control. He writes, "The tinkerer is free to engage in this kind of rummaging. Especially in young adulthood, the institutional constraints that might prevent it are absent. The directives given by one's parents are fewer. One's circle of friends is wider and one's knowledge of the world is wider. The structure provided by schooling, teachers and the regime of adolescent cliques is gone."[2] And, by the time emerging adulthood ends you've substantially got religious things figured out. So, the twenties is the time of life to tinker.

Seeing emerging adults as tinkerers explains some things. For example, it explains the conflict that one of them recently had with her parents. One of my former students was raised in a faith tradition that believes the use of instrumental music in worship services is prohibited by certain biblical texts. She accepted this through her teenage years, yet during emerging adulthood she abandoned that belief and in fact affiliated herself with a church that uses musical instruments in worship. Her parents were offended, hurt, and disappointed by their daughter's decision, and would frequently bring the subject up to try to dissuade her. In fact, it has become a recurring source of conflict between them. When my former student explained this to me, she said, "The more I thought about it the more I concluded that using musical instruments isn't a salvation issue; it's just a tradition. I don't see anything wrong with it." In classic tinkerer fashion, she visited a few churches that routinely use musical instruments in their worship services to see what it was like. She discovered that she rather enjoyed those services, which only provided her more evidence to support the conclusion to which she had been leaning. It's important to note two things here: First, though tinkering with this specific issue, she accepted nearly every other aspect of her parent's faith and practice. Second, her parents saw such tinkering as inappropriate; to them, tinkering wasn't an option.

The parents' reaction points to another dimension of emerging adults' tinkering, namely that tinkering frequently creates tension. Parents sincerely believe that the religion passed on to their children is of a character that it ought to be accepted in toto. Religious authorities have a vested interest in insuring the continuity of religious beliefs and practice so deviations are frowned upon. Beyond the specific issues is the notion that we are not simply talking about tinkering with farm machinery or opinions; we are talking about tinkering with truth, something which ought not to be tinkered with. So, it comes as no surprise that when emerging adults tinker, parents easily get nervous and religious authorities might feel threatened. Realizing that emerging adults are tinkerers raises several important questions: In what ways do they commonly tinker with their Christian faith? What are the consequences of such tinkering? Ought they to be tinkering with their faith at all? It is to these questions that we now turn.

Does Anything Stay the Same?

Before outlining the differences between emerging adults and their older and younger religious counterparts, it might be helpful to acknowledge the ways in which emerging adults' beliefs and practices are not all that different. After all, the notion of tinkering implies that something of the original is retained. When examining the most recent research, one comes away with a clear, more-balanced picture of emerging adults' thinking on religious matters.

What follows is a review of conclusions that can be drawn from the social scientific research on emerging adults' religious life. Those conclusions may be at odds with your own experiences or the people you know. In fact, that's to be expected. Social science research deals with the aggregate, seeking to study enough people to make generalizations based on sound research methodology and statistical procedures. Sociologists aren't trying to explain any one, specific individual; instead, they are simply saying that certain things have a high probability of being true of the members of a particular group. For example, research into the loss of religious faith finds that those with an intellectual orientation (i.e. they are highly intelligent and feel that everything must make logical sense) are more likely to fall away than those who lack such an orientation. That doesn't mean that John (who has such an orientation) will fall away; it just means that he's more likely to do so. When explaining this to my students I often say that when you put a particular person's name into the mix, all bets are off. So, as you read on, resist the urge to say to yourself, "But that's not how it is for my son/daughter/grandchild/friend." Instead, recognize the complexity of God's created humans and the limits of human knowledge. Now, on to what we know.

It is often feared that emerging adults' tinkering will result in them moving away from orthodox views of Christian faith to unorthodox ones. As the parent of an emerging adult said to me as he dropped his son off at the Christian college where I taught, "Don't let our son go off the deep end. We sent our son here [to a Christian college] because we are worried about all of those 'progressive' influences." Those parents and others can rest easy;

the weight of research concludes that emerging adults are no more likely to adopt unorthodox Christian beliefs on fundamental issues than are any other age group. In summarizing numerous studies regarding core Christian beliefs, Robert Wuthnow states: "It does not appear that young adults are less orthodox in their beliefs than they were in the past or than people are now who were young in the past. Nor is there evidence that people with non-orthodox beliefs have become more secular, at least in their views about the Bible. This also seems to be the case for beliefs about Jesus."[3] However, this does not mean that there are not some changes in emerging adults' Christian beliefs.

Make Your Own Religion

One of the most enduring images in the Christian faith is of Moses coming down from Mount Sinai with a tablet of stone in each hand. Those tablets contained the law by which God's people were to live, written by the finger of God (Exodus 31:18). They were called to abide by *all* of it, rather than picking and choosing which portions of it suited them (Deuteronomy 26:16). In fact, in later years God's people blended their worship of him with elements of worship to the gods of Moab, Ammon, Philistia, and other surrounding nations, a practice which greatly displeased God (Jeremiah 16:11). From the beginning it was understood that there was God's truth and then there was everything else. The two were to be kept separate. And, truth was to be taken as a whole, rather than accepted in portions. Though an inadequate analogy, religious belief and practice might be likened to dinner at a friend's home at which, out of deference to the one providing the meal, you ate whatever what placed in front of you without complaint. It would be unthinkable to say, "I don't like that" or "I refuse to eat that!"

One of the biggest differences in emerging adults' religion is that they see it as if it is a cafeteria. At the cafeteria, you are not a treasured guest or even a family member; you are a consumer. At the cafeteria, you are able to pick and choose from among a wide variety of offerings as suits your moods and taste. Perhaps you would like baked cod today and roast beef tomorrow, or chocolate pie but not green beans. Emerging adults are more likely than any other group to approach religion that way, picking and choosing, mixing and matching religious ideas from a smorgasbord of options.

For example, some research finds that nearly six in ten emerging adults believe that many religions may be true.[4] And, about half of all emerging adults believe that one does not have to accept religious beliefs as a whole, that it is okay to pick and choose from among different religious beliefs to fashion a complete set of beliefs.[5] In comparison, a smaller proportion of teenagers (37%) hold such views.[6] One researcher seems to accurately sum up how emerging adults see religious beliefs when writing, "People should use and take what is helpful in religion, what makes sense to them, what fits their experience—and they can leave the rest. There's no need for religion to have to all hang together as one coherent package of belief and lifestyle. Ultimately, religions consist of a lot of accumulated beliefs and rituals that different people have made up for different reasons, which may or may not be relevant to today."[7]

One emerging adult that I met at an academic conference well illustrates this sort of thinking. A graduate student, he was browsing a table of academic books about the study of religion, which led to a conversation about our mutual interest in religion. When asked about his own religion, he replied, "It's a little of this and a little of that. Actually, it's mostly Christian, with a little Buddhism and Kabala mixed in. I see truth in many religions." I asked several of my former students to comment on the practice of selectively accepting religious beliefs and one of them wrote: "I do think my generation is more likely to pick and choose our religion. It just doesn't make any sense to believe that you have to accept everything. I think that God's truth is bigger than our religions. You can find truth anywhere."

Why do emerging adults think this way? Let's return to sociologist Jeffrey Arnett. He believes that part of it has to do with emerging adults' desire to think for themselves. As he explains, "One reason the beliefs of many emerging adults are highly individualistic is that they value thinking for themselves with regard to religious questions and believe it is important to form a unique set of religious beliefs rather than accepting a ready-made dogma."[8] In addition, the tendency to tinker and the need to form their own identity reinforce the need to think for themselves, which in turn produces syncretism of religious beliefs.

Another reason for emerging adults' syncretism is their view of religious truth. Jesus made it unmistakably clear that he spoke religious truth. In John 14:12 he says, "I am the Truth" and no less than twenty-six times in Matthew's Gospel and twenty-seven times in John's Gospel Jesus says, "I tell you the truth." However, emerging adults ask the same question Pontius Pilate asked in John 18:38, "What is truth?" Their answer is, "Who knows?"

Of course, the cafeteria approach perplexes and worries many adults. If religious beliefs are Truth with a capital T, then substituting some of it with something else or discarding portions of it entirely represents a serious problem with grave ramifications. Furthermore, those older than The Twenties see religious pluralism and syncretism as prime evidence that emerging adults have forsaken all religious authority. This is partially true, for if they held to traditional views of religious authority, then they wouldn't be as quick to mix and match beliefs. However, it is more accurate to say that emerging adults have not rejected religious authority altogether; they have merely diluted the notion of a *sole* religious authority and supplemented it with the notion of *multiple* religious authorities—which, as we saw in previous chapters, they may ignore anyway!

Emerging Adults and Evangelism

From a young age I was taught that all Christians are subject to the Great Commission as recorded in Matthew 28:19 where Jesus tells his disciples: "Go and make disciples of all nations, baptizing them in the name of the Father, the Son, and of the Holy Spirit." Do emerging adults believe in the necessity of evangelism to the same extent as others? Significant evidence shows that they see evangelism very differently. Surveys have consistently shown that, in general, emerging adults are more likely than their counterparts to see religion as matter of personal choice and therefore something that is not to be forced upon others. This thinking is reflected in a *Religion and Ethics* newsweekly. When asked to agree or disagree with the statement, "It is important to spread my faith," about half of emerging adults agreed, while 70% of those older than forty agreed. When asked to agree or disagree with the statement, "It is important to convert others," just over one-third of emerging adults agreed while half of those older than them did so.[9]

To illustrate, an emerging adult told me, "People have to choose for themselves. Most people know about Jesus; at least in America. He's not unknown to them. Let them come to you. You shouldn't go around forcing it on them. If they want to go to church, they'll find one on their own." Sociologist Nancy Ammerman calls this "Golden Rule Christianity." It reflects the idea that since one ought to treat others as you would be treated, one ought not to try very hard to proselytize.[10]

What accounts for emerging adults' relative lack of enthusiasm for evangelism? Perhaps it is related to their view of religious truth. You'll remember that previously we noted that emerging adults often do not see religious truth as absolute. However, Christian evangelism is fundamentally rooted in the idea that there is a single path to salvation, expressed in the Bible in passages such as John 14:6 where Jesus says that no one comes to the Father except through him, or 2 Thessalonians 1:8-9 where Paul says that those who do not obey the gospel of Jesus Christ will be shut out from his presence. If the claim of Christian exclusivity is abandoned, then the need to evangelize evaporates.

Given all that has been said about emerging adults' views of religious authority and the role of personal experience in understanding faith, it should come as no surprise that The Twenties are less likely to believe that Jesus is the only path to salvation or that Christianity is the only truth. In his book *Souls in Transition: The Religious and Spiritual Lives of Emerging Adults*, sociologist Christian Smith summarizes emerging adults' beliefs on different religions: "It's fine if different religions want to emphasize specific customs, beliefs or ceremonies, if some people want to do that. But none of the particularities of any religion, emerging adults think, are really that important or valuable about it. Those things are external and incidental. They help give each religion its own culture. But what really matters about religion are the core principles that are shared across religions—belief in God and basic morals."[11] Emerging adults "live and let live" philosophy removes a primary impetus to be evangelistic. While there are certainly many emerging adults who do share their Christian faith, the attitude that motivates such endeavors seems to be weaker when compared to those at another point in life.

Note that not all emerging adults de-value evangelism. Emerging adults who identify themselves as evangelicals are actually *more likely* to believe that it is important to spread their faith and convert others than any other group.[12] This is perhaps explained by observing that for highly devout emerging adults evangelism is proof of an authentic faith. I recently had a conversation with several emerging adults who attend my church in which such feelings were articulated. One told me that he felt that today's churches are too isolated from the lost and too geared toward insiders. "Even the language we use make it hard for the unchurched to feel comfortable" one observed. Another said she felt that churches ought to dedicate more of their resources to evangelism. Yet another bemoaned the fact that too many churches seemed to be on the defensive rather than the offensive. Such comments once again reflect the diversity and complexity of emerging adult attitudes toward Christian faith.

"I'm Spiritual but Not Religious"

Another key difference in emerging adults' Christian faith concerns how they see themselves as religious people. To illustrate, let me tell you a story. One of my former students was raised in a solid Christian home. From an early age she did all of the things that proud Christian parents hope their children will do: enjoy church and Bible class, form strong Christian friendships, attend all sorts of Christian youth activities, live a godly life, attend a Christian college, develop a reputation as a well-grounded person of substantial faith, marry a Christian spouse, and continue to attend church regularly. Yet a few years later, in her mid twenties, things began to change. The church attendance became less frequent. The firm commitment not to drink any alcohol shifted to social drinking (though never to excess). The friendship circle also changed with non-Christians from work filling her social calendar more than Christians from church. People at church soon started to notice that she and her husband were not attending church anymore. Word filtered back to me, and since I have known her and her husband since their college years, I contacted her to "check in" and see what was going on.

Our conversation occurred entirely through messages batted back and forth on the social networking Web site Facebook, which is a miserable way to carry on any sort of substantive conversation. After the first few exchanges ("How are you doing?" "What's new in your life?"), the messages turned more serious when I asked the question I often do when conversing with emerging adults who are my former students: "So, how's your faith?" Oddly, there was no reply for several days, and though I hoped the delay was due to the busy pace of life, I feared it represented something worse. And I was right. When she finally did reply (after another prompting message), she said that it took so long to answer because she was trying to figure out how to answer my question. Then she said, "The best answer to your question is that my faith has changed. I'm still deeply spiritual; I'm just not religious." She went on to explain that she was disenchanted with church, seeing too much superficiality and hypocrisy there. Whereas it was once important for her to be involved in church-based programs and ministries, those were now absent in her life. However, she vehemently denied that she had lost her faith. In fact, she claimed that she "was more spiritual than ever before."

Clearly my former student desired to make a distinction between being "spiritual" and being "religious." Is my former student alone in this or is she merely giving voice to a mindset that permeates her peers in emerging adulthood? I recently asked a church leader for his thoughts on this matter, and he responded by saying, "I think they all think like that." Another of my former students who is himself an emerging adult heartily agreed. The research is more mixed. For example, there is research suggesting that two-thirds of emerging adults feel that personal experience is of better use than church doctrine to understand God; only half of those who are older believe so.[13] This preference for personal experience paves the way for a "spiritual but not religious mindset." Other research classifies emerging adults into those who are religiously involved (e.g. attending church) or religiously uninvolved. About 50% of emerging adults are religiously uninvolved, yet of that group 60% say that spiritual growth is important to them.[14] This pattern suggests that they may well be trying to hold the tension between "spiritual" and "religious."

However, if you get beyond the comments of specific individuals and ask The Twenties as a whole if they see themselves as "spiritual but not religious" a different picture emerges. Christian Smith's study of several thousand emerging adults found that on average only 15% of The Twenties would say that they are spiritual but not religious, and 40% say that such a description doesn't fit them at all.[15] It is true that more of The Twenties say they are spiritual but not religious than do teenagers, but still the overall number is quite small.

What of those who claim to be spiritual but not religious? Do their lives actually reflect that they are living out that sort of a Christian faith? Are the emerging adults who have jettisoned the external/religious vibrantly embracing the internal/spiritual? Sadly, the research suggests that, while emerging adults may claim to be spiritual but not religious, in practice you cannot separate the two. The best evidence here is once again Christian Smith's extensive compilation of research on the religious lives of emerging adults. After exhaustive study of this issue he concludes:

> Little evidence supports the idea that emerging adults who decline in regular external religious practice nonetheless retain over time high levels of subjectively important, privately committed religious faith. Quite the contrary is indicated by our analysis. The

emerging adults who do sustain strong subjective religion in their lives, it turns out, are those who also maintain strong external expressions of faith, including religious service attendance. Most emerging adults, by contrast, who significantly reduce their external religious participation also substantially reduce their subjective, private, internal religious concerns.[16]

[handwritten marginal note: Is the issue the church? Is that when asked?]

In fact, less than 7% of those in Smith's study who claimed to be spiritual but not religious actually lived a religious life reflecting that. If their church attendance dropped off, so did their prayer life. If they were uninvolved at church, they were less likely to say that religion was important to them.

The net result is that the research suggests that you are either spiritual *and* religious or neither. Or, as Smith says, "It simply happens quite infrequently that emerging adults sustain high internal but simultaneously fall to low external religious forms and practices. It is true that external forms of religion tend among emerging adults to drop at more substantial rates than internal forms. But as a reliable broad generalization for most emerging adults, religious life appears to be an all-or-nothing proposition."[17]

Still in the Wilderness

This chapter confirms the assessment offered earlier: emerging adults are struggling to make their way in their Christian journey. Their tinkering and reformulation of Christian faith can be taken in several ways. You might be tempted to throw up your hands in frustration and disgust and say, "They need to get with the program!" I have certainly seen that reaction among many of my middle-aged peers. However, I am not sure that's a helpful reaction. Instead, a more helpful reaction is to say, "Okay, they are obviously struggling to sort out their Christian faith. How can I walk alongside them so as to guide them out of the wilderness and into the clear?" This is a potentially more fruitful response, and certainly one likely to be better received by emerging adults. It seems either hard-hearted or short-sighted to simply leave people to wander in the wilderness. And so, rather than giving up on emerging adults we can link hands with one another and go into the wilderness and retrieve them.

Discussion Questions

1. In what ways have you noticed emerging adults tinkering with their Christian faith? In what ways is such tinkering beneficial? In what ways is it harmful?

2. What's the best response to emerging adults' "cafeteria approach" to religion?

3. Is it realistic to expect emerging adults to develop an enthusiasm for evangelism?

4. In what ways have you seen emerging adults adopt the attitude that they can be "spiritual but not religious?" How ought one best respond to such beliefs?

5. Given everything said in this chapter about emerging adults' Christian beliefs, is there any reason for hope?

Emerging Adults' Christian Life

A n older gentleman shook his head as he scanned the crowd at his church one Sunday morning. With a heavy sigh he said, "I guess religion just isn't very important to young people any more." His comment reflects a rather common perception, especially among older adults, that emerging adults are somehow less religious than other age groups. While each of us could muster our examples to affirm or deny his observation, perhaps a more helpful question to ask is, "What does the research show?" That is, rather than basing our assessments of emerging adults' Christian faith and life on anecdotal evidence, we ought to base such claims on objective social scientific research. Doing so would allow us to avoid the pitfalls of drawing conclusions on narrow, inaccurate, or biased information.

As a college teacher trained in and teaching knowledge discovered through the social sciences, I am a staunch believer that such methods are valuable in helping us understand human beings. Of course, my religious faith reminds me that social science research can never offer a complete picture of human beings; humans created in God's image are far too complex for that, especially when it comes to religious faith! However, I believe that the social sciences can make valuable contributions to our intrinsically limited understanding of the humans God created. Therefore, this chapter provides a snapshot of emerging adults' Christian faith as captured by the most recent social science research. In doing so, it relies heavily on the thoughts and research of one of the premier sociologists studying emerging adults' religious faith, Christian Smith. His groundbreaking work is the most comprehensive research to date, and it provides invaluable perspective on emerging adults' Christian faith and practice.

Religion's Importance

Not long ago, the headlines in my local paper read, "Young Less Affiliated, not Less Believing." The accompanying newspaper story described a report released by the Pew Forum on Religion and American Life recounting some of their research on Americans' religious faith. The headline-grabbing section of the report featured the statement that in 2009 more than one-quarter of Americans ages eighteen to twenty-nine have no religious preference or affiliation, making them "the least religious generation among Americans alive today."[1] Such news inevitably produces hand-wringing and finger-pointing among concerned Christians. And, if that were all there was to the story then we should all be deeply troubled. But that's not all there is to the story. The same newspaper article went on to point out that those same eighteen to twenty-nine year-olds have a belief in the existence of God and the power of prayer that is nearly as strong as that of young people in earlier generations. This may seem confusing, so let's try to untangle the seemingly tangled strands of emerging adults' Christian beliefs and practices.

Let's start with this: emerging adults are not as a group hostile toward religion. One of the largest surveys of emerging adults found that 58% of them said that religion was either quite important or very important in their life.[2] Fifty-five percent of them said that religion is important in their daily lives.[3] And, 78% said that God or some higher power watches over them or guides their life.[4] Another large-scale study of emerging adults' religious beliefs concluded that over 60% of them are in some way religious.[5]

While such numbers are encouraging, it helps to put them into some perspective. Unfortunately, doing that is somewhat discouraging. For example, compared to emerging adults, a greater proportion of full adults say that religion is important to them.[6] And more emerging adults than full-adults say that religion is not at all important to them.[7]

Religious Affiliation

A larger proportion of emerging adults than other ages groups are unaffiliated with any religion. One study reported that 26% of emerging adults were not affiliated with any religion while only 13% of those in their forties were unaffiliated.[8] Furthermore, a sizeable number of The Twenties are not affiliated with any faith tradition because they have left the faith in which they were raised. In one study, fully one in five emerging adults say they were raised in one faith tradition but now don't claim affiliation with any religious faith.[9] In examining the results of a national survey of emerging adults, one researcher concluded: "In all of this, there is a general trend toward considerable disaffiliation from religious traditions and a significant growth in the proportion of American emerging adults who identify as not religious."[10]

Such disaffiliation stems in part from a propensity of emerging adults' to describe themselves as religious, but resist claiming an affiliation with a particular faith tradition. As one of The Twenties said to me, "I don't think of myself as belonging to any denomination. I'm just a Christian." Another said, "When Jesus looks at us he doesn't see labels. All he sees is our hearts. In my heart I know I'm a Christian. He knows I'm a Christian. That's all I need to be." Another emerging adult told me, "We're the ones drawing lines, not God. Denominations are man-made things that only divide us." Research supports such sentiments, finding that emerging adults profess less strong allegiance to a particular faith tradition than do other age groups. In one study, barely more than a third of emerging adults claimed a strong allegiance to their faith tradition, while nearly 60% of those their parents' age did so.[11] Such evidence reveals an underlying sentiment among emerging adults that one's identity is not linked to social institutions (e.g. faith traditions or particular churches), but to self designations (e.g. I'm just a Christian).

A related phenomenon is the propensity among emerging adults to switch faith traditions. Between 28% and 50 % of youth in various religious traditions studied in one investigation had switched from one to another religious category during the five years between being teenagers and emerging adults.[12] Another study found a 20% rate of mobility between faith traditions.[13] Certain faith traditions are more affected by this trend than are others. For example, the proportion of emerging adults affiliated with the Churches of Christ declined .1% from 2002-2003 to 2007-2008, while the proportion affiliated with Baptist churches or "just Christian" churches declined 3.4% and 7.3% respectively.[14]

These migrations pose significant challenges to churches. Since today's emerging adults are less "brand loyal" to a specific faith tradition, they feel free to sample other faith traditions. Knowing this, many churches may be tempted to try to shape their worship or programs to maintain the allegiance of whatever emerging adults remain in that church and prevent the church's teens from migrating when they become emerging adults. At first glance this might make sense; after all you either please the customer or lose him. However, upon further reflection such a strategy seems misguided. For starters, such a strategy places churches in an escalating competition with one another, a sort of never-ending arms race. In this climate some will inevitably not be able to keep up because of limited resources. In addition, emerging adults' migration is usually less a product of a particular church's or faith tradition's identity than it is a product of "where the emerging adult is" during those years. If they're not happy in your faith tradition, then they're not likely to be much happier in the next one either. A sizable number of emerging adults find that the grass isn't always greener on the other side of the hill. In fact, many even return to their original faith tradition at a later point in life. Frankly, the more ominous concern is that an emerging adult will leave the faith tradition in which he/she was raised as the first step toward disengaging from Christian faith altogether. Indeed, this pattern is a common one.

This movement among faith traditions is most likely a result of emerging adults' tinkering in an attempt to commit to the sort of religious faith that they deem the best fit for themselves. However, Sharon Parks offers another intriguing possible explanation. She reminds us that the cornerstone of emerging adulthood is experiencing unprecedented freedom, and yet in the midst of that emerging adults retain (at least at a latent level) their need for older, wiser role models. Parks believes this makes emerging adults more susceptible to the influence of charismatic, dynamic people because such people present the possibility of playing the role of informal guide as one navigates emerging adulthood.[15] Therefore, switching faith traditions may be in part facilitated when an emerging adult encounters a charismatic person in another faith tradition. This would seem to fit the experiences reported by several of my former college students who switched churches in part because they were enamored with the preacher or another strong personality in the faith tradition briefly sampled. One such student said, "I started to go to [X] church because the preacher was really cool. He was laid back and seemed to speak right to me." Another said, "The first time I visited the church I was embraced by several people my own age. They were super-friendly and invited me out for coffee. They seemed to really want to get to know me."

Religious Practices: Prayer, Bible Reading, and Church Attendance

Research also shows that emerging adults are comparatively less likely to engage in certain individual religious practices. For example, 74% of Americans in their sixties and 62% of those in their forties say they pray daily whereas only 41% of emerging adults claim to do so.[16] About one in four of emerging adults spend some time each week in quiet time religious thought whereas almost half of those their parents' age do so.[17] And, they read the Bible daily at half the rate older adults do.[18]

Of course, one of the most visible and significant of all facets of religious faith is church attendance. Though more will be said about this later, the research is clear: emerging adults attend church far less frequently than do other age groups. This conclusion is supported by nearly every major research project undertaken in the past five years. For example, the Pew Forum's Religious Landscape 2010 survey of emerging adults found that one-third of those under age thirty said they attended worship services once a week; 41% of those over thirty said they did so.[19] Results of the large-scale General Social Survey and the national Survey of Youth and Religion finds that 30% of emerging adults attend religious services "regularly" while 55% never attend or attend only once or twice a year.[20]

When examining church attendance rates, we find that some categories of emerging adults are more likely to attend church than are others. Research finds that unmarried men are the least likely emerging adults to attend church, with fewer than an eighth of them attending weekly religious services.[21] Also, regardless of gender, emerging adults who are married are more likely to attend church than those who are single.[22] The relationship between marriage and church attendance and other aspects of religious life is explored in greater detail in subsequent chapters of this book.

Emerging Adults in a Slump

The past few pages have presented a flurry of statistics. When one takes a step back, what does one see? The discouraging conclusion is that the Christian faith of the American teenager is likely to erode during the emerging adult years. Regular church attendance drops by 25%.[23] Fewer than one in ten emerging adults is involved in any activity other than attending worship services on Sunday, a steep decline from the teenage years.[24] Christian Smith sums it up this way: "Most sociological measures of religious practice, salience, and belief also decline over these years. More objective and public religious practices such as religious service attendance decrease in a particularly conspicuous way. Subjective aspects of religiosity such as belief in God and importance of faith decline somewhat less dramatically.

The importance and practice of religion generally declines between the age periods of 13-17 and 18-23. Some or even many American youth go into something of a slump during these years."[25]

Perhaps even more troubling is evidence that such declines in Christian practices are apparent even among those who in their teen years were most religious. In reviewing the available research, Smith concluded, "The teenage group that underwent the greatest amount of extreme change was the Highest Religion category—one in four High Religion teenagers moved to either the Minimal or Lowest Religion categories by emerging adulthood.... Moderately religious teenagers are the most likely to shift to a different level, with well more than half becoming less religious and one in five becoming more religious."[26]

What accounts for this? Christian Smith summarized the available data and found that those teenagers who were the most religious in high school only to become the least religious during emerging adult years had some combination of several things in common:

- They lacked strong parental and non-parental ties to religious faith.
- They prayed and read scripture less frequently.
- They had fewer religious experiences.
- They harbored unaddressed doubts about their faith.[27]

Smith also notes an odd disconnection between what emerging adults observably *do* with respect to their religious faith and what they *perceive to be true* with respect to their religious faith. He writes: "Most emerging adults themselves report little change in how religious they have been in the previous five years. And those who do report change are more likely to say that they have become more, not less religious."[28] In other words, if you ask emerging adults to assess the quality and quantity of their religious faith, they will tell you that they are doing fine. But if you examine the enactment of their faith objectively you'll see a decline in their faith since their teenage years.

Is There Any Way to Keep
Emerging Adults' Faith Intact?

Thus far, we have painted emerging adults' Christian faith as fragile and rather unhealthy. One might be tempted to conclude that emerging adulthood is a large rock formation lurking beneath life's waters poised to shipwreck all those who come its way. Yet as you've read the past few pages you might have been thinking, "Wait a minute! I know several emerging adults who have retained their faith, if not grown in their faith. How do you account for them?" Well, the fact is that some proportion of emerging adults does avoid the rocks under the water and not only survives but actually flourishes during emerging adulthood. Smith's observation is that "A little more than half of emerging adults remain quite stable in their levels of religious commitment and practice or lack thereof.... A certain proportion of highly religious teenagers remains highly religious as emerging adults, as do significant groups of moderately religious and not very religious teenagers."[29] The key questions are whose faith is most likely to grow and what is most likely to bring about an expansion of an emerging adult's faith?

In Matthew 13, Jesus tells the Parable of the Sower in which he describes how different kinds of people receive the gospel. The parable seems to accurately capture the categories of emerging adult faith. First, Jesus says that some of the seed fell on the path and birds arrived quickly to eat it. This seems to correspond to emerging adults who claim no religious affiliation, about a quarter of all emerging adults. Next, some seed fell among rocky places where, despite its initial attempts at growth in shallow soil, the plant quickly dies when scorched by the rising sun. Meanwhile, other seed is scattered among the thorns which choked the young plants as they grew. These two types of seeding seem to reflect the experience of a good portion of emerging adults who demonstrated some faith in their youth and teenage years, only to have it fall by the wayside as they enter emerging adulthood. As we have seen, there is clear evidence of at least a partial decline in emerging adults' Christian faith. Finally, some of the seed fell on good soil allowing a thriving plant to produce a bountiful crop. True to Jesus' words, contemporary research finds that some of emerging adults are actually thriving in their faith. Furthermore, that research has been able to identify some elements which contribute to a greater likelihood that an emerging adult's faith will thrive. In other words, we have a fairly clear idea of what ought to be in the soil.

The first element is parents. Sociologist Gordon Allport draws a distinction between genuinely religious parents (which he calls intrinsically religious) and parents whose religious faith is shallow, immature, and often "in name only" (which he calls extrinsically religious). Emerging adults raised by intrinsically religious parents are significantly more likely to develop and carry a religious faith into adulthood.[30] This is also consistent with biblical commands for godly parents to raise their children to faith (Deuteronomy 6:7, Ephesians 6:4). The reason for the strong effect of parental influence is two-fold. First, parents provide the starting points for a child's understanding of the world. These starting points provide a sort of presumption of validity until replaced by some other understanding of the world. Therefore, the better job parents do of deeply rooting these starting points the more likely those understandings are to resist replacement later. Second, parents also provide their children with a continuous statement as to the true worth and seriousness of Christian faith. As parents live their lives each day what they *do* is communicate to their children whether what they *say* is really true. Every day in hundreds of small and large ways parents model for their children whether religious faith is truly life-transforming (intrinsic) or whether it is merely expedient and compartmentalized (extrinsic).

So how do these two observations fit into the research about the erosion or maintenance of emerging adults' religious faith? The next few lines may seem harsh, so hold on. I believe that most Christian parents have done fairly well when it comes to formal religious instruction (i.e. encouraging church attendance, getting kids to Bible class, supporting involvement in church youth programs, teaching biblical morality). However, I believe that fewer parents than we think are themselves intrinsically religious; their faith is weak or immature and that is exactly what is passed on to their children.

Much evidence supports this conclusion, as sociologists have been unable to substantiate a link between formal religious instruction received as teenagers and a vibrant faith as adults.[31] Jeffrey Arnett's recent research specifically on emerging adults found the same thing, forcing him to conclude: "Certainly there are cases where children grow up to hold the same beliefs as parents, but such cases are too rare to show up in the statistical analyses of groups because it is much more common for children to hold different beliefs from their parents by the time they reach emerging adulthood."[32] This would make sense if the Christian faith which the children inherit from their parents is insufficiently strong and genuine to withstand the inevitable changes that emerging adulthood brings them as we have outlined in previous chapters. In essence, the seed of religious faith is sown on shallow, rocky, thorn-infested parental soil more often than we think. That might be uncomfortable to admit, but it seems to be true.

Research also suggests that it's not only the parents' faith that matters. The quality of the relationship between parents and children during the teen years is also a factor influencing emerging adults' Christian faith. Previous research has found that when parent-child relations are strained, the children are more likely to abandon their Christian faith in later years.[33] More recent research specifically studying emerging adults confirms this,[34] and this too is in line with biblical warnings about maintaining familial harmony (Ephesians 6:4). Perhaps the significant amounts of conflict present in such strained relations operate at cross-purposes to the parents' goals of instilling lasting faith in children. Or, it may be that when parents and their children do not get along well, one way for an emerging adult to passive aggressively act out against parents is to abandon the religion in which they were raised. Regardless, though some degree of conflict between teenagers and their parents is inevitable, it behooves parents and children to do everything possible to minimize or contain it lest it become a detriment to the children's religious faith in later years.

The second element contributing to healthy emerging adult faith is internalization, which refers to the process of genuinely incorporating one's faith into their everyday life. This is a particularly important characteristic, as Christian Smith's research points out. He devised a way to measure the internalizing of religious faith and found that when a teenager scored in the top quarter percentile on this measure he/she has an 85% chance of landing in that same top quarter percentile as an emerging adult. In other words, a teenager who manifests a genuine, internalized faith is highly likely to retain that through his/her twenties. In contrast, those teenagers scoring in the lowest 25% on internalization have *less than one percent* chance of landing in the top 25% as emerging adults. Of course this makes sense, plus it is biblically sound for this is the sort of genuine faith of which the Bible speaks (Matthew 22:37-39). The challenge is to determine what brings about this internalization of faith, and on this count opinions vary; suffice it to say that it varies from person to person and that it is most likely a combination of several things. But it seems clear that when *something* occurs that encourages emerging adults to internalize their faith they are more likely to maintain that faith.

The third element contributing to solid Christian faith among emerging adults is practice, that is, habitually engaging in outward yet personal expressions of faith. Smith notes that when teenagers pray and read the Bible regularly they are more likely to continue those habits as emerging adults.[35] Such practices reinforce the faith commitments already made and create a hard-to-break habit. Plus, they are in line with clear statements in the Bible linking such activities to faith (e.g. Luke 18:1, Ephesians 6:18, 1 Thessalonians 5:17).

Christian Smith offers one intriguing explanation as to why such practices might drop off during the emerging adult years. For emerging adults raised in a Christian home, they associate the faith they have learned with their childhood and their parents—two things emerging adults are trying to distance themselves from. He explains: "The religion in which emerging adults were raised is connected with an earlier phase in their lives when they were dependent on their parents. Independent persons do not keep doing things that belong to their earlier dependence. Therefore, learning to stand on one's own two feet means, among other things, getting some distance from one's family's faith and religious congregation."[36] So, reading the Bible, praying, and engaging in other Christian practices may fall off as emerging adults pursue their quest to craft their own identities. In contrast, Smith also notes that religious practices such as prayer and Bible reading might continue into emerging adulthood precisely *because* they help maintain and reinforce their Christian identity.

(4)   The fourth element is adequately addressing the doubts an emerging adult might have regarding his or her religious faith. In his book *Faith and Doubt*, John Ortberg observes that nearly all Christians experience doubts about some aspects of their faith at some point in their lives.[37] The Bible seems to agree since it includes stories indicating that even Jesus' disciples Peter (Matthew 14:30-32) and Thomas (John 20:24-31) experienced doubts. My own research into the subject has found that those who have fallen away often point to irreconcilable doubts as chief influences in their apostasy.[38] The same appears to be true for emerging adults as studies conclude that the presence of unresolved doubts is linked to the erosion of their faith.[39]

How doubt is handled is crucially important. Many emerging adults whom I know have recounted to me that they felt ashamed for having doubts. And, despite the Bible's encouragement to be merciful to those who doubt (Jude 22), many told me stories of how they felt stigmatized by other Christians when they had the courage to voice their doubts. In addition, many expressed frustration that those with whom they shared their doubts were unable to knowledgably respond to their questions. I cannot overstate how important it is to respond with gentleness and patience (and all of the other fruits of the Spirit listed in Galatians 5:22-23) when conversing with emerging adults who are in the midst of doubt. When anyone expresses doubt, his/her circumstance must be impartially acknowledged, taken seriously, met with a Christ-like response, and addressed with solid, biblically-grounded replies. In fact, research finds that if those who fall away from the faith are more likely to return if they experience such responses to their doubts.[40]

The final element that's associated with bringing about healthy faith among emerging adults is regularly having religious experiences during the teenage and emerging adult years. Of course, religious experiences are highly subjective things, but this notion includes having had prayers answered and feeling the strong presence of the Holy Spirit in one's life. Such experiences have the effect of validating one's religious beliefs from something "outside of yourself" and therefore become potentially powerful ingredients in cementing one's faith—somewhat like Jesus' miracles did for those who observed them (John 2:11, 7:31, 11:45). Plus, such experiences make faith more real, reliable, and important to Christians.

Different . . . and Similar

If Henry Ford were to see the automobiles of today he would be amazed. Things have certainly advanced since the days of the Model A and the Model T. Cars are bigger, faster, heavier, and certainly come with a lot more options than Ford could ever have imagined. Some things Ford knew well, such as the hand crank, would be gone. Yet surely he would recognize the four wheels and the steering wheel. A windshield would not be unknown to him. And while much of what's under the hood looks radically different, the essential principles of the combustion engine have not changed. And that's the point: though today's car looks a lot different than those of the early twentieth century, at their core they are still cars. Likewise, emerging adults' Christian beliefs and practices are in many ways different and all too often diminished when compared with those of their older Christian peers. However, alongside those differences is the realization that the foundations are the same.

DISCUSSION QUESTIONS

1. What material presented in this chapter surprised you?

2. As you consider the review of emerging adults' Christian life presented in this chapter, what most alarms you? Why?

3. This chapter claims that fewer parents than we want to admit do the job they ought to in order to successfully pass on their Christian faith to their emerging adult children. Do you agree with this?

4. Internalization is a key element in developing more vibrant Christian faith among emerging adults. How can that be attained?

5. Now that you have read this chapter, what specific recommendations would you make to your church? What recommendations would you make to families? To emerging adults?

5

Emerging Adults
and Church

I admit I was a little sleepy. It wasn't as if I had stayed up late the night before; I had simply run a few more miles than usual the day before and my body needed a few more hours of rest. However, each Sunday morning the elders and ministers of the church I attend meet together prior to worship for an hour-long time of prayer followed by another hour's discussion of pressing congregational business. Though I teach college courses full-time, I also serve the LORD as the every-Sunday preaching minister for my church and so I attend those early morning meetings. After going around the room in heartfelt prayer, the floor was opened up for any of the four staff ministers to share news or concerns with the group. One of my ministerial colleagues, who volunteers his time working with emerging adults, snapped me out of my sleepiness when he abruptly made this statement: "I'm concerned that there may be a mass exodus from the congregation among our young marrieds and singles." I turned my head his way and listened closely as he summarized his conversations with many of the emerging adults attending our church. He recounted conversations over dinner tables, at coffee houses and around the campfire, each with a remarkably consistent theme: "We are struggling with church."

I stared at the floor and, frankly, missed the next few moments of his comments because I was lost in my own thoughts. Many of those with whom he spoke were my former students, and I knew them well. I was heart-sick, partly because of the distressing news he brought and partly because what he was sharing was identical to what I had been hearing for several weeks in my own conversations with several emerging adults. It only confirmed what I already knew in my heart to be true: emerging adults are indeed struggling with church. This chapter outlines emerging adults' views on church (or as they often phrase it, "organized religion"), noting how different their view is from both those older and younger than they.

It's Not the Color of the House . . . It's the House

"Struggling with church." What does that mean? If we were to be honest, most Christians sometimes struggle with church. We certainly struggle with people at church. Far too many Christians have seen the hypocrisy of their fellow believers. Others have encountered racial prejudice, doctrinal paranoia, or mean-spirited politics. Some have been hurt intentionally or otherwise by those who claim to be brothers or sisters in Christ. If we were to be even more honest, we would acknowledge that all too often church services and Bible classes are boring. We would confess that we often drag ourselves to church with low expectations wishing that we were somewhere else. And while emerging adults surely struggle with these sorts of issues, they are certainly not the first, nor will they be the last. These are familiar struggles, and I suppose that this side of heaven they are not likely to go away. However, when emerging adults say that they are "struggling with church" they mean something deeper and different. Perhaps this story might help us understand.

Several years ago, I heard a man describe his mid-life crisis. He explained that for several months he had been restless, feeling as if his work was meaningless and his relationships were hollow. He said that he came home to the same house every night and complained to his wife about something that he didn't like. One night it was the color of the family room walls. The next night it was wear on the hallway carpets. After that he griped about the scratched appliances in the utility room, the peeling paint in the pantry, and the small crack developing in the ceiling. Whenever he would complain about such things, his incredibly patient wife would say, "We can always replace the carpet" or "Let's re-paint the family room next weekend, if you like." In reply, he would always dismiss her suggestions saying, "Oh, never mind!"

Finally, after going on a tirade about how he didn't like the drab color of the house's exterior, his wife offered to get estimates as to what it might cost to repaint the house. Her husband exploded in a raised voice and shouted, "It's not the color of the house . . . it's the house! I don't want to live in this house anymore! I don't want to live in any house anymore!" With a confused look on her face, his wife asked him what he meant by that. Her husband said he wasn't entirely sure himself. All he knew is that he didn't think that changing the house's color, carpets, or appliances would help.

To make a long story short, the husband convinced his wife to join him in "living off the grid" which for them meant purchasing a cabin in the woods far from civilization and making do without electricity or running water. You see, the man was certain that modern Americans had gotten away from their true roots with the land and had settled for a sham existence dependent on the creature comforts of the twenty-first century's developed world.

Emerging adults are not unlike the man I have just described. They too have looked around their world and found something to be seriously lacking, only it's not their house—it's the church. And, just as repainting the house wouldn't cut it for the man in the midst of mid-life crisis, eliminating the hypocrisy, boredom, and staleness of church will not appease emerging adults. Their struggle with church runs much deeper than that. It's not the color of the house; it's the house itself. In other words, emerging adults aren't just questioning what Christians do in their churches; they're questioning the need for and worth of church itself.

Several conversations with emerging adults whom I know reflect this deeper struggle with church. One of them told me, "You don't have to go to church to be a Christian. Jesus never actually specifically says that we have to go to church. If it was so important, wouldn't he have said so?" Another wrote to me saying, "I'm 'churched-out.' I went to church *all the time* I was growing up. I no longer see the need to anymore." An older emerging adult who had not been to church in over seven years said, "I feel a little guilty about not going to church and my parents still give me grief over it. But it's where I am right now. You can't force people to go to church. That's dumb!" And, another of my former students confided in me that she has no problem with someone going to church. She continued, "If they're getting something out of it, that's great. But I don't get a lot out of it so I don't go." These comments shed some light on how emerging adults see church. But they also suggest that emerging adults views on church are simple: they don't like it. However, that's too simplistic. In fact, emerging adults' views on church are quite complex and untangling them is a mighty task.

Who Needs Church?

One immediately noticeable difference between emerging adults' views of church and those of older adults is that emerging adults simply do not see church as central to the Christian faith. Whereas two hundred, one hundred, fifty, or even twenty years ago most Christians would have seen Christian faith and church attendance as inextricably linked, emerging adults see them as two completely different things. For them, you don't need church to be a Christian. Church is at best optional and at worst expendable. This viewpoint was well captured by a minister friend of mine who said of emerging adults, "They're skeptical of church." What he meant by that was that they're skeptical that church is as necessary as it has always been claimed to be. Or, as one of my former students once flippantly observed, "Maybe church is like your tonsils."

What is going on that leads emerging adults to see church as unnecessary? Certainly one contributing factor is their belief that one can be spiritual but not religious, a notion explored previously. However, at least for those emerging adults who were raised in Christian homes, another related factor might be at work. Called the personalization of faith, the notion here is that at the most fundamental level God seeks relationships with individual people. The choices to believe in God and live a life that reflects God's will are all *individual* choices, not corporate ones. Like many emerging adults, I had it ingrained in me growing up that on the judgment day we will all face God alone and give an account for our lives (Romans 14:12, 1 Peter 4:4-5). I was reminded that neither my parents nor the religious group I affiliated with would yield my salvation (Matthew 16:27, 2 Corinthians 5:10). That was up to me. In this sense, all religious faith is personal. In addition, the past thirty years have seen a renewed emphasis on a person's personal relationship with God. I have heard and preached many sermons exhorting Christians to develop such a relationship. Ironically, all of this emphasis on individual choices and personal relationships with God may have had the unintended effect of leading emerging adults to diminish the need for anything else when it comes to their faith. Jeffery Arnett puts it this way: "Emerging adults tend to personalize their relationship with God in a way that makes participating in organized religion unnecessary or even an impediment to the expression of their beliefs."[1]

Another explanation for emerging adults downplaying the value of church is that it is a way of asserting their individuality. As we saw previously, emerging adulthood is a time when people are engaged in a search for a lasting identity. It is a time of life when they seek to act as individuals, free from previously experienced constraints. To that extent, emerging adults see church as an infringement on their individuality. As Arnett says, "To most emerging adults, participating in a religious institution, even a liberal one, requires them to abide by a certain set of beliefs and rules and therefore constitutes an intolerable compromise of their individuality."[2] Participating in church life inevitably requires one to sacrifice some individuality. The Corinthians discovered this when coming together to share the Lord's Supper (1 Corinthians 11:17-22). The Romans discovered this when integrating Jewish and Gentile believers into one community (Romans 14:1-15:7). And, the Bible consistently calls Christians to make such sacrifices for one another (Romans 12:10, Philippians 2:3-4). Thus, setting aside one's individuality is nothing new. What's new and challenging is navigating these changes in the midst of the upheaval of emerging adulthood.

The Dysfunctional Church

It's not only that emerging adults see church as unnecessary, they see it as dysfunctional. Much has been written in the past decade about emerging adults' disenchantment with church, and so here I will only briefly review that line of thought. Two of the most widely read books are Dan Kimball's *They Like Jesus but Not the Church* and David Kinnaman and Gabe Lyons' *Unchristian: What a New Generation Really Thinks About Christianity . . . and Why It Matters.* I would encourage you to read either or both of them for a more detailed picture. Their conclusions are in line with numerous other recent research projects identifying a pervasive negative attitude among emerging adults toward churches, their leaders, and their adherents. Those books and a myriad of other sources also substantiate the reasons why emerging adults have come to hold these views. Many have had negative experiences with church, experiencing first-hand hypocrisy, discrimination, hyper-judgmental people, betrayal, and disappointment. Others reject church because of the unfolding sexual, political, and financial scandals in which religious leaders and institutions are often involved. Even for those who remain active in churches, there is what Arnett calls a "wariness" of religious institutions.

Close students of the Bible and the history of Christianity will recognize that these sorts of problems are nothing new. First-century believers struggled with sexual immorality (1 Corinthians 5:1), theft (John 12:4-6), internal conflict (1 Corinthians 3:3), and hypocrisy (Galatians 2:11-13). Things didn't improve much in the centuries following as the historical record details identical problems up to and including the present day. So, it's not that such things are new; today's emerging adults aren't the first group to experience dysfunctional churches and Christians. But today's emerging adults may be more sensitive to it than previous generations. Psychologist Bob Altemeyer believes that emerging adults' skepticism towards church merely reflects a larger trend toward holding all social institutions in lower esteem.[3] Indeed, the past decade has seen highly visible scandals featuring political and religious leaders and organizations so it stands to reason that emerging adults might see churches as "another brick in the wall" and question their credibility and necessity.

However, one must be careful not to paint too dire a picture. In the midst of the doom and gloom view of emerging adults' attitudes towards church comes two encouraging signs. First, some research finds that emerging adults' negative views towards church might be overstated. In his summary of a large swath of emerging adult research, Christian Smith concludes, "Most emerging adults seem positive about organized or mainstream religion in the United States. Most have respect for, are positive about, and are not personally turned off by it."[4] How can this be in light of what was said above? Smith seems to suggest a distinction between "organized religion" and "religious people," finding that most emerging adults (up to 79%) positively view mainstream religion in the abstract sense, while a sizeable number of them (over two-thirds) hold negative views about religious people who are overly hypocritical, judgmental, or angry. It may well be that emerging adults see value in churches in the ideal sense, but are turned off by them in their application. Second, as Smith notes, "The vast majority also have positive feelings about the tradition in which they were raised."[5] Perhaps this is what social scientists call a Third Person Effect, in which someone believes that something is not true of them or the people they know, but is true of everyone else (the Third Person). So, it may be that an emerging adult feels that he/she is not a hypocrite and that no one he/she knows at church is a hypocrite, but a lot of other Christians are.

A Sense of Belonging

One of the more popular television programs in the 1980s was *Cheers*. Set in a bar in Boston, Massachusetts, the series followed the exploits of the bar's owner, his employees, and the crew of regulars who seemed to practically live at the bar. The lyrics to the show's opening theme song seem to apply quite directly to emerging adults:

Making your way in the world today takes everything you've got.

Taking a break from all your worries, sure would help a lot.

Wouldn't you like to get away?

Sometimes you want to go where everybody knows your name,

and they're always glad you came.

You wanna be where you can see our troubles are all the same.

You wanna be where everybody knows your name.

These lines point to a deep need that we all have to be affiliated with a community of some sort. They speak to a common desire to feel as if we fit in somewhere. They imply our need for acceptance and camaraderie. They give voice to our need as humans to feel as if we belong. *Cheers* suggested that such needs could be met at a bar. For Christians, such needs ought to be met at church. Sadly, emerging adults don't feel as if they belong.

The Greek word for "church" is *ekklesia* meaning "the called out"; it is most often used to denote an assembly of people with common cause,[6] and so it is not incorrect to say that the people *are* the church. From the earliest of times, Christians have found other believers (i.e. the church) to be a source of great comfort, blessing, and fellowship (e.g. Acts 2:42). It remains so today. Nearly everyone I have ever met who remains associated with a particular church does so because of the people who compose that group. Even among emerging adults I know, those who have found a church with which to identify say that they chose that church because of the people there. As one remarked, "I can't imagine worshipping anywhere else. The people are so genuine and supportive. They're like my family." Another, worshipping elsewhere, said, "If it weren't for the people my husband and I wouldn't be here. The people here are the best!" Yet another told me in all confidence, "The Bible classes are not the best and I wish it were closer to where we live. But we've made many good friends here and that's the number one reason we stay." Conversely, my conversations with emerging adults indicate that people are also the chief thing that repels them from churches. One wrote me a note explaining, "My roommate and I tried several churches in the area, but none of them were too friendly." Another said, "After college, I thought I would go to church in the church where I grew up back home. But there wasn't anybody there my age so I started going to church somewhere else where there were more people my age." I believe that the church I attend is a very friendly place filled with lots of people of all ages. But one of my former students, in her twenties, visited several times and never returned saying, "It wasn't that friendly." Research finds that connections with people are consistently among the top reasons why people choose to attend a given church.[7]

What's the point of all this? People matter. Or to put it differently, Christians have "people needs." And it seems that for emerging adults people are especially important. One of my former students, an emerging adult and a life-long Christian, raised in a Christian home and devout in her faith, related this story to me. Since her husband was out of town, she came to church services one Sunday morning alone. When she arrived she scanned the crowd as they settled in for worship but couldn't find any of her friends. Alarmed, she frantically looked for someone else among the four hundred attendees that morning with whom she felt comfortable sitting. Finding no one, she hastily exited, got into her car, and drove home.

Ethan Watters claims that since emerging adulthood features social interactions weighted towards interactions with similar-circumstance peers, friendships are especially important for emerging adults.[8] He notes that they place greater emphasis on "Urban Tribes," circles of friends that play highly significant roles in their lives and even become a sort of surrogate family. And, with the advent of social media such as Twitter and Facebook, the emphasis on friendships is bound to continue. It seems safe to say that if emerging adults feel as if they have friends at a church then they will go to church. However, if they feel they don't have friends, then church attendance falls by the wayside.

And in that simple calculus the church often comes up short. The fact is that emerging adults don't feel as if their "people needs" are being met. Robert Wuthnow researched the extent to which people of different age groups feel as if they have friends at church. His conclusion is quite clear: "Young adults are much more likely than older adults to have few or no friends in their congregations. In fact, among those in their twenties, 65 percent have five or fewer friends and 27 percent have no friends in their congregations."[9] That means that less than one in ten emerging adults has more than five friends at church! Christian Smith addresses this condition by observing,

> If an emerging adult wants to go to religious services somewhere that they like or join in with some religious group, that's fine. But that is not likely their place of real social belonging. They belong when they hang out with friends, at college or at a job they like, maybe visiting family. But do emerging adults feel a strong sense of belonging in any religious congregation? Nah, not really, actually not very much at all. . . . At best they go to religious meetings, probably enjoy them well enough, are friendly with the people there, and then leave, heading off to more important things.[10]

This is interesting because in Smith's previous research on the religious faith and lives of U.S. teenagers he found that most of them felt quite connected to friends at church.[11] And Smith found that many emerging adults in his research who don't feel a sense of belonging at church *are the same ones who participated in the earlier research in which they claimed to feel some sense of belonging at church.*

Why don't emerging adults feel a sense of belonging at church? The answer to that question is complicated. Part of it has to do with the fact that there are typically comparatively fewer formal programs or structures in place that might attract emerging adults. As one of my former students said of one church she attended for a few weeks before moving on, "I didn't stay there because there was nothing for me there. I tried another church because I heard they had a singles ministry, but that turned out to be false. Their 'singles ministry' was just one church member getting some people together every few months for dinner." My former student experienced what has previously been mentioned: When it comes to intentional programming and focused attention, there's a lot for teenagers but not as much for emerging adults.

Another reason emerging adults feel disconnected is that they seem to lack what I call *joining skills*. To illustrate, let me tell you about the time immediately after I married. My wife and I moved hundreds of miles away to another state where I would attend graduate school. Since we were both diligent Christians and church was important to us, we were placed in the position of needing to find a place to attend church in a strange, new city—a situation in which emerging adults commonly find themselves. We dutifully visited a few churches, sampled their worship services, and were even invited into some people's homes. After a few weeks, we chose a church and jumped right into congregational life.

In this transition, my wife and I had to muster the courage to walk through the door of an unfamiliar church building where we knew no one. We had to endure the awkwardness, uncertainty, and stress that accompany new social situations. We had to stick with it even though it was difficult and offered comparatively higher costs than benefits. Each of these actions make up *joining skills*, for they are the kind of things one must do to become a church member. I believe they are skills, which implies that some have them and some don't; some do them better than others; and they can be taught and learned.

Having taught in college for over twenty years and met literally thousands of emerging adults during that time, I am convinced that emerging adults seriously lack *joining skills*. For all of their bravado about seeking independence and making their own way in life, I have found that many (if not most) lack the courage it takes to walk through the door of an unfamiliar church. Despite the importance that they place on interpersonal relationships, many (if not most) do not have it in them to make the investments it takes to ride out the initial difficulty and awkwardness of getting to know a new church. We have certainly emphasized the need for them to join a church in their emerging adult years, but I believe we have not equipped them to do so. This may be because we believe that such education isn't necessary; after all, *we* did it without having *joining skills* taught to *us*. Or it may be because we're uncertain how to teach such skills. For whatever reason, the skills are not being taught and I believe they ought to be.

The implications of everything said above is clear: Christians *must* reach out to emerging adults at their churches so as to forge relationships with them, and emerging adults *must* make themselves available for and invest in those offered relationships. Notice that I place the responsibility on individual people, not structures. Churches could surely facilitate relationship building through programs geared to that end. However, at the end of the day it falls on people to follow the New Testament's command to practice hospitality (Romans 12:13), carry one another's burdens (Galatians 6:2), have all things in common (Acts 2:44), and love one another (1 John 3:11). The fact that doing so is awkward, difficult, and intimidating ought to be irrelevant. The stakes are too high and the solutions too simple not to do so.

Church-Hopping and Church-Changing

I am a dinosaur. When I drive my truck around town, I listen to the radio. Yes, the radio. When I am not listening to the sports radio station on the AM band (a technology unknown to emerging adults), I listen to music on the FM band (a technology barely known and derisively viewed by emerging adults). That alone makes me a dinosaur, but there's more. When I listen to the radio, I do not continually jump between radio stations seeking better programming. If a commercial comes on, I listen to it. If a bad song comes on, I stick with it hoping that a better one will follow. I suppose you might say that I am a loyal listener. Of course, this behavior is quite unlike what I've observed among emerging adults. Whenever I ride in their cars I notice that they run their iPods through their car stereo system, playing the music they want to hear. If they ever do listen to the radio, their fingers seem to always be working the buttons to scan for stations playing a better song. I suppose you might say that emerging adults are transient listeners. In my experience it works the same way with churches. Emerging adults are far more transient in their approach to church than are older adults.

Sociologists have long noted that American Christians have a consumer mindset, and much has been written about how more and more Christians are church-shopping, most of it uncomplimentary.[12] Emerging adults often find themselves church-shopping; but in a highly mobile society like ours, plenty of older adults do too. What's different is that emerging adults are not merely church-shoppers. They are church-hoppers. Robert Wuthnow describes church-hopping this way: "Church hopping involves staying in the market, or perhaps better, tinkering with several possibilities rather than settling down with one."[13] More tellingly, Wuthnow's research finds that of the emerging adults who regularly attend church about half sometimes attend at other churches and another 16% say they do so regularly.[14] This fits the experiences of many emerging adults with whom I have communicated recently. One e-mailed me about her spiritual life, indicating that she bounces between as many as four different churches, depending on her mood. Another told me that she regularly attends a church somewhat far from her home, but when she stays up late on Saturday nights she attends a different church closer to where she lives. Needless to say, older adults exhibit far less frequent church-hopping.

There are likely numerous reasons for emerging adults' inclination to church-hop. Part of it is expediency. Part of it may reflect the lack of *joining skills*. Part of it is also related to marital status; research shows that among emerging adults single people are much more likely to church-hop than are married couples.[15] Part of it is also related to an observation made by someone working with emerging adults at my church. He noted that, when it comes to church, emerging adults vote with their feet. Unlike previous generations, they don't stick around a church to complain in hopes of changing the congregation. They simply move on to another church.

But does church-hopping matter? Given emerging adults' underwhelming rates of church attendance, perhaps we ought to be content that an emerging adult is attending church anywhere. However, I believe that emerging adults' church-hopping is problematic. The Bible teaches that Christians are to encourage one another (1 Thessalonians 5:11, Hebrews 3:13, 10:25), which presumes some sort of community in which this can take place. Church-hopping lessens the likelihood that someone will form the sort of relationships with others that give rise to Christian encouragement. This isn't to say that encouragement can only come from an established church-based relationship. Yet experience teaches that it is more likely to come about when one is associated with a tight-knit faith community. The Bible also calls us to a life of ministry (James 2:14-26). Again, strictly speaking one does not need to be an invested member of a church to enact ministry. Still, experience teaches us that being a part of a church makes it more likely that people will do so, if for no other reason than that structured opportunities are offered. Church-hoppers miss out on such opportunities and, despite what they want to believe, they are less likely to be involved in Christian service. Similarly, the Bible calls Christians to continual growth and maturation in faith (2 Peter 3:18). Though not necessary for spiritual growth, an abiding commitment to a church makes it more likely to occur. Christian Smith's research on emerging adults found that, of those whose faith grew during their emerging adult years, one thing they had in common was the nurturance of adult figures in their local congregations.[16] Finally, church-hopping emerging adults are less likely to develop the kinds of friendships that are so crucial to their Christian faith.

Church-hopping contributes to another phenomenon that I have noticed among emerging adults: a lack of a sense of place. By this I mean that many emerging adults feel as if they are uncertain as to where they fit in at church. They're not sure what their role is. As stated previously, they're too old for the teenage group, yet they feel little affinity for the adults in their thirties and forties. It's true that emerging adults who are married typically feel a greater affinity toward older adults, yet that still leaves the sizable number of unmarried emerging adults without such a perceived connection. Most of the people they see teaching Bible classes at church are older or married. It seems (at least to them) that they're not as often sought out for participation in worship services or inclusion in other ministries. They tend to receive fewer social invitations for dinner and other activities.

Emerging adults with whom I have spoken frequently ask the question, "Where exactly do I fit in at church?" In response to my queries on this topic, one wrote, "I'm not sure what I'm supposed to be doing at church. I don't see any way to get involved, and no one is knocking on my door to ask me to be involved." Another explained that, "It's not like they won't let me do things at church. They just never ask me to." But it doesn't have to be this way. I have noticed this dynamic at work: an emerging adult makes a commitment to a particular church, which is followed by some indeterminate amount of time during which the emerging adult is sort of "on probation." During this time people from the church are getting to better know the emerging adult; trust is built as it becomes evident that the emerging adult is not a short-timer and credibility rises as the emerging adult is able to prove himself/ herself. At some point, if the emerging adult sticks around long enough (and makes some overtures), he/she begins to slide into a comfortable role. Church-hopping short-circuits this process because when emerging adults church-hop they're not around long enough to make the kind of invest-ments that result in securing a discernible role at church.

Concluding Observations

I close this chapter with a handful of observations. First, it becomes clear that if we are not careful a pattern of negative reinforcement is all too easy to create. Emerging adults value church less and are wary of its dysfunction. So they stay away. Churches, seeing fewer emerging adults, naturally focus more of their energies on teenagers and married families which they have in greater abundance. This means that when emerging adults overcome their lack of joining skills and make it to church they feel as if they don't belong and find it difficult to see what their role at church might be. So, they pull back. In turn, churches are uncertain what to do with these emerging adults whom they never seem to be able to please or keep in large numbers, so they gripe about the paucity of emerging adults and their relative lack of faith. Emerging adults see this which only confirms their initial suspicions that church isn't valuable and the cycle starts over again. If this is the case, then both churches and emerging adults must make some changes in order to break the cycle.

Second, when it comes to emerging adults and church attendance, there's a notable difference among groups. Females are more likely to attend church than are males. In fact, research finds that females make up two-thirds of the emerging adult churchgoers.[17] This is typically explained by the fact that women of all ages demonstrate greater levels of religious faith and activity than do males, which may be because it has been suggested that in America female gender roles are more in line with Christianity than are male gender roles.

Research also finds that church attendance rates rise as one moves through the emerging adult years, with those in their later twenties attending more often than those in their early twenties.[18] These differences suggest that, insofar as church is concerned, some emerging adults are likely to be at greater risk for negative outcomes than others.

Discussion Questions

1. Parents and church leaders often feel helpless when they consider emerging adults' views on church. To what extent are they really helpless to influence emerging adults' views?

2. How would you explain to an emerging adult who is skeptical of the importance of church attendance the need to make church attendance and involvement a priority?

3. How might your church increase emerging adults' sense of belonging?

4. Does the Bible offer any specific scriptures or principles to help address emerging adults' views on church?

5. What specific recommendations would you make to your church to address the material in this chapter? What recommendations would you make to families? To emerging adults?

6

Emerging Adults
and Their
Relationships

For some reason, kids like to tease each other (or at least boys do!). I vividly recall the day at my elementary school when some of my second grade friends and I noticed that one of our pack, Ted, was sitting at the girl's table for lunch. There were actually two or three tables of boys and two or three tables of girls, but since the numbers didn't work out evenly there was always a table at which both boys and girls sat. Of course, you never wanted to be so unfortunate as to sit at that table; it just wasn't done.My friends and I noticed that Ted sat at that table two days in a row. Worse, he seemed to do so on purpose, going to the back of the lunch line which practically insured he would get stuck at the mixed gender table. Worse still, he sat next to one of the girls in our class, Mindy, both days—and he was smiling as he talked with her.

Of course, we had to tease him about it, so later that day on the playground I am ashamed to say that I joined in the merciless teasing heaped upon Ted. With mocking, sing-song voices we sang, "Ted and Mindy sitting in a tree, K-I-S-S-I-N-G. First comes love, then comes marriage, then comes

Danny in the baby carriage." Danny was the new kid at school who was dragged into the humiliation because he had the misfortune of being new.

I share this shameful, yet all too common, story as a way of illustrating that from a very young age we are subtly taught that there's a sort of natural order to love, sex, and marriage. It's reflected in the song we used to tease Ted. The song presupposed that romance is for those of opposite genders. It reaffirmed that those romantically involved like being by themselves. It clearly demonstrated that there's some physical contact between the two before marriage, which is, in fact, normal. And it also implied a lot more intimate sexual contact after marriage resulting in childbirth (even if we didn't quite know how the babies came about!). In short, the song provided a glimpse of what normal romantic relationships look like.

If emerging adults were to write a song providing a similar glimpse into what they believe is normal for romantic relationships today, it would likely be very different. That's because emerging adults have come to see love, sex, and especially marriage in some markedly different ways from those who came before them. Talking with emerging adults about issues of love, and marriage often reveals conflicting views. Yet clear patterns can be seen. For starters, romantic relationships are keenly important to emerging adults, but they are viewed and managed rather differently than they used to be. Today's emerging adults tend to follow a different path from singlehood to marriage than did their parents.

Then there is their attitude toward marriage. As a group they have come to hold attitudes toward marriage that are strikingly divergent from those held by previous generations. More alarmingly, they significantly depart from their predecessors when it comes to sexual attitudes and practices; fewer of them see marriage as the prerequisite for sex. That emerging adults see issues of love, sex and marriage differently from previous generations is plain to see. What it means is less clear. But one thing is crystal clear: Notions of love, sex and marriage are also important to the Christian faith and emerging adults' views on these matters often puts them at odds with traditional Christian views, thus posing a challenge for all concerned.

"I want to get married... I guess. I mean I do... sort of... mostly. It's just... scary."

The words above haltingly tumbled out of one of my students' mouths as we were sitting on a bench in the surprisingly warm early spring sun. She was enrolled in my Marriage and Family Communication class, a course which never fails to spur out-of-class conversation. She had come to me seeking some advice as to how to deal with twin troubles which had recently entered her life: her parents' back home were separating after twenty-some years of marriage and her boyfriend attending another college had just ended their relationship. Our conversation turned from the specifics of those two situations to her apprehensions about marriage in general. She sighed and said that marriage was something she wanted for herself; in fact she dreaded the thought of ending up alone in life. But she was in no hurry to get married. There was school to finish and jobs to find. Plus, marriage scared her . . . a lot. "What if I marry the wrong guy? What if I marry him and he changes? What about divorce?" she said. My twenty plus years of teaching college students has led me to conclude that such questions are on the minds of many emerging adults. As one of my twenty-something former students told me recently, "Everyone I know is all about relationships. They're all trying to play it cool, but, trust me, it's all about relationships." In that context the word "relationships" means "romantic relationships."

At first glance, that would seem to be okay. After all, Christianity has always prized romantic relationships. The Bible is replete with stories in which people like Jacob and Rachel meet and fall in love. It recounts the institution of marriage in Genesis 2. It describes healthy marriages in Ephesians 5:22-33 and 1 Peter 3:1-7 without covering up unhealthy marriages like Nabal and Abigail's (1 Samuel 25:1-44). It speaks to dimensions of the marital relationship ranging from in-law relations (Genesis 2:25) to monogamy (Hebrews 13:4) to divorce (Matthew 19:1-12). In short, to borrow a phrase from Frank Sinatra, marriage and Christianity "go together like a horse and carriage."

And it's not just that the Bible has some things to say about marriage. Research has concluded that marriage is absolutely the most crucial influence on most adults' Christian faith. Whether or not you marry, when you marry, who you marry, and whether or not you have children play a larger role in the health, quality, and character of one's Christian faith as an adult than any other factor.[1] Church attendance is just one example of this. Large scale studies of church attendance patterns consistently finds that married adults of all ages attend worship services more regularly than do those of the same age group who are single.[2] This is significant because it helps explain why it is that emerging adults attend church less frequently than do those who are older; emerging adults are marrying later *and* because fewer emerging adults are getting married.[3] In fact, some researchers believe that this explains virtually all of the observed differences in church attendance rates among emerging adults now and forty years ago.[4]

How do emerging adults see marriage? They are certainly not hostile toward marriage, nor have they dismissed out of hand the notion of being married. Indeed, research finds that upwards of 90% of all emerging adults say that they plan to marry eventually.[5] Of course, we previously noted that "eventually" ends up meaning a significant postponement of marriage, at least when compared with previous generations. Still, emerging adults see marriage in their future. One breezily posted to her Facebook page, "Someday the marriage boat will stop for me, but not anytime soon!" Another said to me, "I'd like to get married, but not for awhile. There are too many things I want to do first. Finish school. Travel. Get my career going." Yet another responded to my inquiry about his current marital status saying, "Not married yet. Not looking. Not worried. All in God's time." And they do marry. Fully 75% of all Americans are married by age thirty, and another 15% will marry after that.[6] Research finds that the range of ages at which Americans first marry has become so spread out that emerging adults now consider it "normal" to be well into the thirties and yet be unmarried.[7] Still for emerging adults, turning thirty often marks a psychological line which once passed indicates a heightened need to start getting serious about finding a mate. As one researcher put it, "So in theory they can get married whenever they want, whenever they decide the time is right, but in practice 30 is for many people a deadline age."[8]

Perhaps the best word to describe how emerging adults view marriage is to say that they are wary of it—wary in the way that someone crosses a frozen pond: tentatively, with one eye on the surface below and one eye on the safety of the nearby shore. One of my students once shared her apprehensions about marriage by telling me that most of the marriages she had seen were in some manner dysfunctional. "If that's what marriage is," she told me, "I don't want any part of it." Another emerging adult, in an e-mail response to a question I raised about wariness regarding marriage, said, "Today's emerging adults absolutely are wary of marriage. I know I am, and so are most of the guys I know. How can you not be? It seems harder to make a marriage work today. And, so many of them fail. What guarantee do I have that I won't be next?"

One reason emerging adults are wary of marriage is because they place so much emphasis on marrying the right person. Of course, this has always been a concern, but it seems to receive greater emphasis now because of emerging adults' propensity to find their "soul mate." A soul mate refers to a person who completes another person, someone with whom one can connect in an extraordinary fashion. In short, soul mates often represent an idealized life partner for each individual. In her book *For Better*, Tara Parker-Pope says that a soul mate is all-encompassing, head-over-heels fulfillment: a best friend, a business partner, somebody to share sex, love, and chores.[9] With a Disney-type description like that, who wouldn't want to marry a soul mate? In one survey of emerging adults, 94% agreed that first and foremost your spouse ought to be your soul mate.[10]

In the many conversations I have had with college students over the years about who to marry, the notion of "The One" or a soul mate has come up so often that I have lost count. But at the same time emerging adults recognize that it's all too easy to marry someone who is not your soul mate. As one said to me, "I live in fear that I'll marry the wrong person and end up like my parents—divorced and bitter." Another admitted, "I am afraid that I will settle, you know? There aren't that many good guys out there and I don't want to be stuck with leftovers." Coming of age in a time of high divorce rates and blended families, it's easy to see why emerging adults might well seek partnership with a soul mate as insurance against befalling the same fate.

While many in the church continue to tussle over divorce as a doctrinal issue, emerging adults are far more concerned about it as a real threat to their life happiness. One of my former students compared the fear of divorce to the fear of cancer. Substantial research indicates that emerging adults whose parents are divorced are more prone to marry impulsively and are more likely themselves to get divorced.[11] Emerging adults have internalized this and it affects how they see marriage.

For committed Christians, this wariness of marriages leaves them in a somewhat conflicted state. They're wary of marriage. But they also feel the pressure to get married because "it's what Christians do." Females also feel the pressure to have children. Though the stigma has been reduced, it's still seen as odd not to be married by thirty. Then there's the pressure to marry another Christian. As one emerging adult told me, "Of course I want to marry a Christian, but I worry about that too. I know a lot of people who did that and it still turned out bad." A twenty-eight-year old single wrote to me saying, "People keep asking me if there's anyone special or when I'm going to settle down. I get sick of it. Maybe it will happen someday, but I don't know when and I don't know who. I do know that I won't be pressured into it."

What conclusions can be drawn from our discussion about marriage? The research is clear: the best way to safeguard an emerging adult's Christian faith and involvement is to get married to a committed Christian. No surprise there. Everyone, including emerging adults, knows this. As Proverbs 18:22 says, "He who finds a wife finds what is good and receives favor from the Lord." Though the average age at first marriage has been pushed back, the fact remains that most Americans are first married in their mid to late twenties. This means that unless they marry their childhood sweethearts, they are most likely to marry someone whom they've met in their twenties. In turn, this means that during his or her twenties an emerging adult had better come into contact with viable prospects for marriage or else opportunities for successful marriage will be missed. In short, a window for marriage tends to open up immediately after high school and begins closing as age thirty approaches.

To take advantage of this window, Christian emerging adults must go where there are other Christian emerging adults who might make viable marriage partners. Since about 60% of all Americans attend college immediately after high school, this means that emerging adults ought to strongly consider attending a Christian college or a secular university where there is a large, vibrant group of Christian emerging adults. Sadly, it too often seems that people's desires to safeguard their Christian faith takes a backseat to other concerns, such as not leaving home, getting the right college degree, or finding a job. And so the emerging adult stays close to home, choosing the local college where there are few if any Christian emerging adults. Or an emerging adult seeks a specific degree at college far away where again there are few Christian emerging adults. I have seen both of those scenarios and many more like them play out over and over again. The bottom line is that emerging adults need to be around other emerging adult marital prospects whether that be at a Christian college, a secular college with a large Christian group, or a church with a sizeable number of emerging adults. As I think about this challenge, I'm reminded of Jesus' words in Matthew 16:26: "What good will it be for a man if he gains the whole world, yet even forfeits his soul?"

This might sound a bit old-fashioned. It is at odds with what Joshua Harris in the mid-1990s called the "gift of singleness." It's even counter to Paul's personal opinion expressed in 1 Corinthians 7:1 that it is good for a person not to marry. Yet the research mentioned above and my own experience persuade me that marriage is so crucial to an adult's Christian faith that it ought to be given top priority. The odds that someone will maintain a Christian faith, continue to attend church, and be active in that church significantly drop when one remains single or marries a non-Christian.

A careful balance is needed here. While there are undeniable benefits to Christian marriage, people shouldn't be pressured to marry. Many emerging adults report such pressure, especially those attending Christian colleges. Wisdom says that to beat emerging adults over the head about getting married will only foster a boomerang reaction. Many emerging adults tell me that they're tired of hearing the subtle or explicit references to "settling down" or "finding the right one" or "making a home." As one said, "Every time I go home my mother asks me if I have met anyone yet or if I am seeing anyone special, and so does everyone at church. I know what they mean by that; and it gets old." So it seems that concerned parties need to pray for the wisdom to know how to encourage marriage to a Christian mate without badgering emerging adults about it.

The Gatekeeper Is Gone

Several years ago, I noticed that one of my students had pinned numerous badges to her backpack. A small, round one boldly proclaimed in white letters on a red background, "I'm Waiting." I was intrigued. What did the phrase mean? What was she waiting for? So, as she filed past me one day at the end of class, I asked her about it. She happily explained that she received the button at a Christian event for teenagers, and it accompanied her signing a document committing her to abstain from all sexual activity until she was married. She noted that the button served as a public display of that commitment and a helpful self-reminder that she had made that commitment. She smiled slyly and said, "It also scares off the wrong kind of boys."

Such programs reflect the firm Christian belief that marriage is the only proper place for sexual activity. Marriage has traditionally been seen as the gatekeeper for sexual activity, precluding such activity prior to marriage but allowing it after marriage. Of course, there have always been and will always be those who ignore the biblical stance on sex outside of marriage. In discussing such matters we run the risk of thinking that the current generation is so much worse than how it was when we were that age, when in reality we weren't so pure ourselves. Still, there's convincing evidence that things have changed significantly. Today's emerging adults hold views toward sex outside of marriage that are drastically different from previous generations, and their sexual activities reveal how different they are. Simply put, emerging adults' sexual beliefs and conduct not only run counter to those articulated in the Bible, they place their spiritual lives in jeopardy.

One look at patterns of emerging adults' sexual activity makes it clear that marriage is no longer a gatekeeper to sexual relations. At the start of emerging adulthood approximately half are sexually active; by the end of emerging adulthood virtually all have become sexually active.[12] Thirty-percent of college students report having had at least one "hook up" (i.e. sex with a virtual stranger).[13] One quarter of all emerging adults have had two or more sex partners in the past year.[14] In one study three quarters of emerging adult men said that their first sexual experience was not in a marital or even a committed loving relationship but an "adventure" or a "rite of passage."[15] While it is true that those professing Christian beliefs exhibit *lower* rates of sexual activity, their rates of sexual activity do not drop significantly.[16] I attended two Christian colleges and have spent over twenty years teaching on college campuses affiliated with Christian faiths. To this day I maintain regular contact with a large number of emerging adults. I can assure you that many Christian emerging adults are sexually active before marriage.

What accounts for this? One explanation has to do with the postpone-ment of marriage. Delaying marriage means that emerging adults have to maintain their abstinence for a longer duration and frankly that's a challenge for them. They too often give in to the barrage of sexual temptations. Another explanation concerns the extent of experiences with relationships. Our culture emphasizes sex while concurrently emphasizing the need to do all that can be done to insure marital success. And so, many emerging adults have come to believe that it is necessary to have previous experience in managing relationships prior to marriage, rather than it being "on the job training" in marriage. Arnett says, "Emerging adults believe they should explore different love relationships; that such exploration is both normal and necessary in order to prepare for committing one's self to a marriage partner."[17]

While all of the above might be true, it begs the question, "Weren't they raised to know better than to engage in sex before marriage?" Of course, the answer to that question is a resounding "Yes!" That message is repeatedly pounded into children and adolescents in Bible classes, at youth events, during summer camps, and even at the dinner table. Children and adolescents also have clear cut accountability structures in place to encourage them to adhere to a biblical lifestyle when it comes to their sexuality. Parents, youth ministers, and peers offer a means to check-up on and somewhat regulate sexual activity during those years. But a curious thing happens when one exits high school: such directed messages largely end. Emerging adults don't hear the message to retain their sexual purity. There are almost no accountability structures available to them; they're typically living away from parents, there's almost never an emerging adult minister, and few emerging adults turn to their peers for accountability in their quest for sexual purity. What arises is a sort of "don't ask, don't tell" arrangement that leaves emerging adults on their own when it comes to staying within God's boundaries. We all too often assume that "They already know that," and so we stop talking about it. In one sense, they do "already know that." However, there are plenty of other things that people "already know" about godly living and yet we don't stop talking about them. For example, we don't stop telling people to love one another as they love themselves simply because "they already know that."

The time has come to put the gatekeeper back in place. Perhaps emerging adults need to be reminded in an age-appropriate manner that they are at special risk from the temptations of pre-marital sex. Such messages might be in the normal routine of special classes for their age group at church, but those are few and far between. Certainly parents can gingerly convey the same message. And some sort of adult mentor might do the same thing. It seems to me that the key is to have what I call "an honest conversation," which means approaching the topic in a manner that directly yet gently states the situation, the risks, and the consequences. It is a conversation that treats the emerging adult like an adult with the respect and concern they are due, while simultaneously making it clear what is acceptable and what is not. As an adult mentor for many emerging adults, I have had such conversations and I believe that they can be effective tools for helping Christian emerging adults to be better disciples of Jesus Christ.

In addition, let me suggest this to emerging adults: it is absolutely imperative that you prevent yourself from being in any situation that sets you up to fail. One of my favorite stories in the Old Testament is the story of Potiphar's wife trying to seduce the handsome young Israelite Joseph. After Joseph has refused her overtures on several occasions, she corners him again, grabbing him by his cloak. Genesis 39:12 says that Joseph "left his cloak in her hand and ran out of the house." Joseph recognized the power of the temptation and immediately removed himself from the situation. Given the powerful temptations associated with sexuality, emerging adults need to increase their odds of successfully resisting temptation by avoiding those situations where their potential for failure is high. This means that even though you are of age, and even though all of your friends are going, don't go to the club. This means that if you live on your own in an apartment and arrange a date with someone, always go to public places and never go back to your place unless there is someone else there in the same room with you. The problem is that emerging adults are often unsuccessful at managing the tensions between adulthood and adolescence. That is, they have some of the trappings of adulthood (an apartment of their own, the ability to go to a club, extensive freedom without immediate accountability), but they face the same enormous sexual desires of a late adolescent.

"I Have Over 1,100 Friends"

At the university where I work, I often teach a class titled Interpersonal Communication, a portion of which discusses research on the role of communication in friendships. One semester, the class went especially well, with the students and I feeling a strong sense of camaraderie and goodwill toward each other. On the last day of class, one of the students approached me and said, "Would you mind if you and I became friends on Facebook?" I replied, "Sure." Then the student said, "Great! You know, I have over 1,100 friends and I'd be honored to add you too." I chuckled and said, "You don't have 1,100 friends. You might know 1,100 people, including me, but they're not your *friends*." With a puzzled look the student said, "Of course they're my friends."

In the same class, we read an excerpt from a book on adult friendship by communication professor William Rawlins in which he claims that "being there" for friends is the chief criterion by which adults measure their friendships. In discussing the reading each time I teach it, I am struck by how many of the college students eagerly agree with Rawlins. Semester after semester they passionately explain how important their friends are to them and how in many cases their friends are the only ones who are "there" for them. As one student shared with me, "Everyone else routinely lets me down. My true friends never do."

Sentiments like this underscore a key reality of emerging adult life: friends are very important. Emerging adults have usually moved away from home, and thus their contact with parents is limited and often mediated (i.e. it occurs via the phone or computer screen), so parents are not really in the picture. Most emerging adults are not yet married, so they don't have a spouse to turn to for companionship and support. What they do have are friends, and they occupy a significant place in an emerging adult's world. In their essay on emerging adult friendships, Carolyn McNamara Barry and Stephanie Madsen offer several reasons why friendships are a crucial ingredient in emerging adulthood.[18] In addition to offering companionship, friends help emerging adults develop their own identity and influence how emerging adults feel about themselves. Friends also contribute to emerging adults' understanding of how relationships work and offer valuable preparation for marriage by fostering the skills to manage intimacy and interdependence.

Research finds that emerging adults look to friends to know how to select behavioral choices and to validate their own behavioral choices.[19] In my experiences on Christian college campuses, I have seen firsthand the influence that friends have on emerging adults. Upon graduation, many of my students have moved into an apartment or house with their friends from college. I have observed that if the Christian emerging adult's roommates make a habit of attending church, then the emerging adult will typically do so as well. But if the friends do not attend worship, then the emerging adult usually does not either. I have observed a similar effect with respect to "clubbing." If on the weekends a Christian emerging adult's friends get dressed up and go to a club for an evening of drinking and dancing, then the emerging adult is highly likely to join in too. And I have seen it often work this way: if a Christian emerging adult's friends act immaturely, then the emerging adult will follow suit.

If friends exert such significant influences on emerging adults, then it becomes vital to consider what kinds of people emerging adults choose to be their friends. Sociologists have long known that "Birds of a feather flock together." That is, people generally form friendships with others who are substantially similar to them. And, generally speaking, Christian emerging adults have a lot of friends who are similar to them. Research finds that about half of a Christian emerging adult's friends are religious, with most saying that their close friends share similar religious views.[20] Of course, this is good news in that it means a large chunk of friends offer the possibility of positive influence stemming from a shared worldview.

However, upon closer inspection an alarming fact appears: Only 17% of an emerging adult's close friends are involved in the same religious group (e.g. at the church they attend).[21] Furthermore, compared to all other age groups, emerging adults are the most likely to say that they have few or no friends at the churches they attend.[22] In fact, 65% of Christian emerging adults who attend church say they have five or fewer friends at church and 27% say they feel as if they have no friends there.[23] One of the more common refrains I hear from emerging adults when talking about churches is "There's nothing there for me." By this they partially mean that the worship isn't what they would like or there is a lack of programs geared to emerging adult needs and interests. However, I have also come to understand that for many emerging adults that phrase also means, "There's nobody there my age to be friends with." Many of my former students have explained to me that they stopped attending church altogether because they simply didn't feel as if they had any friends at church—any church. One said to me, "I don't want to go to church alone." I invited another former student, a late twenties emerging adult who wasn't attending church anywhere, to visit my place of worship. She declined, saying, "I don't know anybody there." "But you know me," I exclaimed. "Yeah," she replied. "But you don't count." (Ouch!) Of course I don't count; I'm not an emerging adult.

This is significant because having close friends at church is a key determinant in whether or not an emerging adult attends or is active in a church. For example, only 15% of emerging adults participate in a group religious activity other than attending worship services, yet the vast majority of those who do claim to have close friends doing so with them.[24] One of my former students is currently bouncing back and forth between two churches, attending worship services and participating in various ministries in both places. She became connected with the first church during her college years, visiting and then committing to the congregation with some of her friends at the time. Now, several years later, she supplements that with her involvement in the second church because that's where her roommate attends and the two of them go together. Another family friend of mine is currently in her first year of college in a city far from home. She desires to attend a church affiliated with the faith tradition in which she was raised. But she's attending a church affiliated with another faith tradition with which she's less comfortable because that's where her new-found friends go.

This discussion of friendship and church carries substantial implications for churches. Though a person might hold the position that one ought to commit to a church because it teaches Truth, or aligns itself with a particular faith tradition," the fact of the matter is that few emerging adults make church a priority in their lives and those that do tend to go where they can interact with other emerging adults. Most are simply not concerned with other things. Thus, churches must become places where emerging adults can find friendship. Yet doing so poses a huge challenge for many churches because they have few if any emerging adults currently among their body. And so, many churches face a dilemma: they need emerging adults to attract other emerging adults, but they lack emerging adults who might serve to attract others .

What is to be done? One approach is an attractional, programmatic model. I call it the "Build It and They Will Come" model, a reference to the film *Field of Dreams* in which an Iowa man is told that if he builds a baseball field in the middle of his corn field the ghosts of past baseball stars will appear to play. In this approach, churches start some sort of program of ministry to emerging adults, get it up and running, get the word out about it, and wait for emerging adults to come. Often someone is hired to oversee the program which might consist of Bible classes, social events, and service events. It's like a teenage youth group for emerging adults. Currently many campus ministries follow this model, as do a few churches with full- or part-time "singles" ministers. While there are many benefits of such programs, they chiefly allow emerging adults to connect with their peers, which as we have seen is a crucial ingredient in emerging adults' participation in church. I believe more churches need to implement such programs. Emerging adults are clearly falling through the cracks of congregational life and programs such as this increase the likelihood that fewer will do so. Many of my former college students tell me that they choose a church because of its program of activities geared toward emerging adults. Closer conversation with them reveals that they were attracted to the church because of the program and through participation in it they found friends and a church home.

Yet churches seem slow to pursue such programs. Perhaps it is due to limited resources or uncertainty as to how to start such programs. Or perhaps it is because emerging adults are notoriously inconsistent in their church involvement. Regardless, I believe that churches need to look beyond such concerns and ramp up their efforts to tend to *all* of the flock, including emerging adults. Implementing formal programs designed to meet the needs of and foster friendships between emerging adults would accomplish this.

While the "Build It and They Will Come" model is one approach (and we certainly need more of it), there is another model that could be followed in order to facilitate friendships and church involvement among emerging adults. I call this the "Snowball" model, referring to the idea that to make a large snowball you start with a small, tightly packed snowball and then begin to roll it in the snow so that snow sticks to it, thus enlarging the snowball as it rolls. In this model, churches start with a few deeply committed emerging adults who through common friendship activities reach out to other emerging adults, inviting them to join them in social activities, acts of service, and church involvement. Over time, this core group increases in size as it builds momentum. Here there is no formal program, no paid minister. Instead, through a sort of "guerilla style" pattern friendships are built and emerging adults are naturally pulled into church involvement as relationships are strengthened. It's not unlike Jesus sending out his disciples two by two in Matthew 10 or the pattern demonstrated throughout Acts where a few people are converted and they in turn draw in others in their social circle.

I have seen this model followed with great effectiveness at the church where I worship. An emerging adult couple became affiliated with my church and made it known that they had a heart for the spiritual health of emerging adults. They immediately began to get to know the few other emerging adults who were loosely associated with the congregation, sharing coffee, dinner, hikes, game nights, and movies with them. As friendships were cemented, other Christians within the emerging adults' friendship circles who were not attending church were pulled into the routine of social activities and were soon attending church too. The growing group expanded outward to take on more formal activities at church such as teaching Bible classes and working in the benevolence ministry. From one couple there has sprung a rather large and diverse group of emerging adults who are all friends with one another and are far more committed to and involved in church. Though that couple would say that they were only offering what they call "simple hospitality" to emerging adults, they were also offering something emerging adults crave: friendship. And, since most of them were raised going to church, it is not alien to them to see church as a place where friendships are fostered. I believe this is what more churches need. They need committed emerging adults who through the "snowball" model leverage emerging adults' need for friendship to get them to recommit to church.

Of course, the problem is that such emerging adults are few and far between. Indeed, my congregation floundered for years when it came to meeting the needs of emerging adults chiefly because there weren't any emerging adults to form a coregroup. To address this problem, church leaders can be more intentional about identifying emerging adults in their congregations and encouraging them to be the sort of snowball starters described above. In essence, they are inviting emerging adults to envision themselves as partners in the church's efforts in discipleship. I have done this two or three times with newly married emerging adult couples. I sat down with them and explained that I saw in them outstanding qualities that would make them excellent snowball starters. I shared with them my dream for what ministry to and with emerging adults could be in their church and asked them to pray and think about such a task. In two of the three cases, the couples did so and soon thereafter began to act as snowballs for emerging adults in their churches. Though challenging, I know it can be done. I know that anything can be done with the Lord's blessing.

One other thought on friendships, emerging adults, and churches. In her book *The Critical Years: The Young Adult Search for a Faith to Live By*, Sharon Parks calls churches "mentoring communities."[25] By this she means that churches can be the sort of places that foster personal relationships between older and younger persons. This is a biblical concept too, for the New Testament speaks of older women forming relationships with younger women (Titus 2:3-4) and recognizes the intergenerational nature of first-century churches (e.g. Titus 2:2, Titus 2:6, 1 Timothy 5:1-2). We too easily assume that emerging adults only seek friendships with other emerging adults and that they are not interested in friendship with anyone older. My experience tells me that this is not the case. Many emerging adults indicate a willingness to participate in friendships with mature adults. Because they often feel as if they are on their own as they transition through emerging adulthood, they're happy when anyone takes an interest in their life and reaches out to them. Furthermore, churches are natural environments in which this could occur; in fact churches are one of the few remaining places in American society where generations regularly mingle and socialize in meaningful ways.

Fully adult Christians ought to make more of an effort to cultivate friendships with emerging adults, inviting them to meals, opening their homes, talking with them after services, and serving alongside them. I can attest that emerging adults offer much in friendship and are themselves blessed by such friendships. So, if you're reading this book and you want to do something immediately to help retain emerging adults at your church, sow the seeds of friendship with one of them. You might be surprised at the increase the Lord will give you.

DISCUSSION QUESTIONS

1. Sometimes we think that the differences between generations are greater than they really are. How different do you think today's emerging adults really are when it comes to thoughts on marriage?

2. "The best way to safeguard an emerging adult's Christian faith is to get married to a committed Christian." How would you respond to that?

3. What can churches and concerned parents realistically do to help emerging adults maintain sexual purity?

4. Given the importance of friends in an emerging adult's life, what can churches do to foster the development of friendship bonds?

5. Sharon Parks mentions that churches can be "mentoring communities." How might that be achieved?

Emerging Adults
and College

Since the end of World War II, Americans have pursued a college education in ever increasing numbers. Indeed, college attendance has become so common that in America today, nine out of ten high school students expect to attend college and about two-thirds actually enter college.[1] Some will move across the country to attend college and others will attend the community college at home. Some will choose a Christian college while others will try the state-supported school. Some will experience dorm life on campus while others will continue to live at home. Some will travel abroad and some will take classes online. Though experienced differently, college dominates the landscape of early emerging adulthood. In fact, as was noted earlier, the rise in the proportion of Americans attending college contributed to the creation of emerging adulthood as a distinct period of life.

The college experience fits well with the interests of emerging adulthood. Arnett expressed it best when he wrote, "In many ways, the American college is the emerging adult environment par excellence. It is expressly designed for the independent explorations that are at the heart of emerging adulthood. . . . College is a social island set off from the rest of society, a temporary safe haven where emerging adults can explore possibilities in love, work, and world views with many of the responsibilities of adult life minimized, postponed, kept at bay."[2] Perhaps this is why the Yale University

Herald observed, "Somewhere along the way, college life attained mythic status in America, whether from high school students dreaming of blissful anarchy or from adults reflecting on 'the best time of their lives.'"[3] Since so many emerging adults experience college in one form or another, let's consider how the college experience influences emerging adults' Christian faith.

College as Exploration

During my years as college professor, I have come to hold several firm beliefs about higher education, some of which have not always been popular among my colleagues. I remember a hallway conversation with two of my colleagues. Since we taught at a Christian college, we wrestled daily with the tensions between the school's academic mission and its spiritual mission. As this conversation unfolded, one of my colleagues said in unmistakably clear terms that students were in college to receive an education and that all other concerns ought to take a backseat to that. I offered a different view, timidly suggesting that much "education" during college takes place outside the classroom and that the ancillary products of college life such as dating, faith exploration, friendships, learning to live away from home (with a roommate), and the like were just as important as the formal education. My colleague vehemently disagreed, yet I held to my position, finally saying, "You and I might disagree, but our students see it my way."

How do emerging adults see college? At first glance you might be tempted to offer the obvious answer: "They see it as the next step in their continuing education after high school." And there's research showing that today's college students see their pursuit of a degree in purely instrumental terms; rather than "learning for learning's sake," they see a college education as the means to attain a good job and all that comes with it.[4] But if you probe a little deeper, you'll get a more complete answer. I asked many of my former college students what college meant to them. Their answers were instructive both for what they said and what they did not say. None of the emerging adults with whom I spoke saw college in purely educational terms. None of them said anything like, "It was the time of my life during which I attained more education." Instead, they said things like: "It was awesome! I had it so good then! I spent 24/7 with my closest friends and had the best experiences of my life." Another said, "College for me was when I got my act together." Another explained that, "College was where I grew up. It was where I decided who I wanted to be."

Such comments capture the chief way that emerging adults see the college experience: as a time of personal and social growth and exploration. I call this the "season of growth and exploration." Research confirms this, with many studies revealing that emerging adults see their college years as a time of accelerated personal growth and maturity.[5] College is uniquely suited to the search for personal growth because most colleges and universities encourage it. Like most other campuses, the university where I teach encourages its students to explore things. Here are some of the phrases lifted directly from the printed material given to freshmen during their orientation to college: "Branch out"; "Try new things"; "Join a new interest club"; "Get to know someone different from you." College students respond to such messages because they make so much sense to them. They're open to new experiences. As one of my current students told me, "I was so ready to leave high school behind and get to college. I'm ready for new things." Another shared with me that she felt constrained during her high school years, with limited opportunities for personal growth. Yet in college she feels that she has been unshackled and is now free to explore a larger world. (And to underscore that fact she said that she and her best friend got matching tattoos last weekend!)

College as Excess

Emerging adults seem to be getting the message, though there's evidence that they also take the encouragement to try new things too far. This I call the "ethic of excess." Research finds that an alarming number of college students indulge in their new found pursuits to excess.[6] From dating to drinking to eating, emerging adults in school frequently demonstrate a lack of self-control, engaging in activities to an unhealthy extent. Romantic relationships often become a distraction and the sexual activities that frequently accompany it are often pursued with abandon. Binge drinking is notoriously prevalent on many college campuses. Entering students are warned about the "Freshman Fifteen," a reference to the common gain in weight students experience from eating too much. Moreover, many emerging adults associate college as a time when it is permissible—and even expected—to walk on the wild side or go off the deep end. The popular singer and songwriter Tom Petty well summarizes many emerging adults' attitudes when he said of college, "You have four years to be irresponsible here. Relax. Work is for people with jobs. You'll never remember class time, but you'll remember time you wasted hanging out with your friends. So, stay out late. Go out on a Tuesday with your friends when you have a paper due Wednesday. Spend money you don't have. Drink 'til sunrise. The work never ends, but college does."[7]

Away from home for the first time and experiencing heretofore unseen freedom, many of my college students simply couldn't control themselves. It is one thing to recognize that since they're not yet fully developed these emerging adults might demonstrate poor judgment. But it is another thing altogether to put such individuals in an environment that preys on such weaknesses and actually makes it more difficult to demonstrate self-control and good judgment. Sadly, American colleges seem to have become such environments.

The "season of growth and exploration" and "ethic of excess" pose stern challenges to emerging adults' Christian faith. When I think about them, I cannot help but be reminded of Jesus' words in Matthew 16:26, "What good will it be for a man if he gains the whole world but forfeits his own soul?" The "season of growth and exploration" opens a window of temptation that in many ways is much larger than in previous years. It's a bit like the story of the Prodigal Son Jesus shares in Luke 15:11-16. In that well known story, the younger son goes to a far away place and engages in riotous living. To import that story's situation into this discussion of emerging adulthood, we might say that the younger son's account is similar to that of emerging adults. Both think they're sufficiently grown up, ready to strike off into the world and explore it. And in fact both have their parent's support to do so. They leave home, and thus the restraints to temptation previously in place (i.e. the parent's home, a familial support network, supportive friends) are removed. Both enter environments filled with temptation experienced in the name of exploration. You know what comes next: the young son succumbs to temptation, hitting rock bottom. And so it is for many emerging adults.

I am convinced that most Christians will face a greater number of diverse and difficult temptations during emerging adulthood than at any other point in their life. They often do so in faraway places, removed from familiar support networks and beyond the reach of concerned parents. They often do so in an environment that explicitly and implicitly says, "Why not?" Research consistently finds that emerging adults are more likely to make good moral choices and maintain Christian beliefs when Christian parents continue to be actively engaged in their life.[8] With the advent of Skype, Facebook, and unlimited cell phone calling plans, it is easier than ever to maintain an intentional presence in an emerging adult's life. Moreover, research indicates that emerging adults desire such involvement so long as it morphs to recognize and fit the emerging adult's new station in life.[9] A family friend of mine parenting three emerging adult children recently observed that we used to think that the parents job ended when their children were out the house. Now, he says such thinking needs to be revised to reflect the reality that a parent's job doesn't end until the children are married . . . and maybe not even then!

The ethic of excess makes it harder for Christian emerging adults to demonstrate self control. Self control is a crucial part of the Christian life. Paul and Peter encourage us to develop it (1 Thessalonians 5:8, Titus 2: 2-12, 1 Peter 5:8, 2 Peter 1:6). Those apart from God are said to lack it (2 Timothy 3:3). Wisdom says that lack of self control leaves us weak and defenseless (Proverbs 25:28). The dangerous thing for emerging adults during their college years is the way college life suggests that the need for self-control can be suspended, allowing college students to essentially take a vacation from saying "No." My experience forces me to conclude that many college students place self-control into the category of things that they are not yet supposed to have attained because they're not yet "real" adults. Moreover, my experience with college students tells me that they are terribly afraid of missing out on the college experience. Not long ago I had a conversation with one of my students about her ever-increasing number of class absences. She explained that she was extremely tired since she usually stayed up until 3:00 A.M. talking with her friends, watching movies, making late night runs to the convenience store, chatting online, or visiting Facebook pages (notice she wasn't doing homework). When I suggested that she forgo some of that in favor of an earlier bedtime in order to get a little more sleep prior to my 9:15 A.M. class, she furrowed her brow and said, "I can't do that. I might miss out on something." When I made a similar suggestion to one of my freshman students several years ago, one of the seniors overheard my advice and later told me, "You can't tell them that. If they take your advice they'll miss out on the best parts of college! The best parts of college happen after midnight." The notion of missing out that pervades much of college campus life threatens to unravel the best efforts of many Christian emerging adults to maintain self-control.

In addition to chipping away at emerging adults' self control, the ethic of excess raises the risk that emerging adults will develop unhealthy or sinful habits during college that will last a lifetime. I know of many students who began drinking coffee during college. I know of several students who took up smoking cigars during college. Other students have developed far more troubling, sinful habits. I know far too many students who moved from experimenting with alcohol to becoming binge drinkers during college. In fact, research finds that patterns of adult alcohol consumption are often established during the emerging adult years.[10] I know far too many students who entered college as virgins and exited after having had multiple sex partners and more permissive attitudes toward pre-marital sex.[11] In an environment that encourages excess, an emerging adult might not only give in to the temptation to be involved with sinful choices previously declined, but may do so with greater frequency and abandon.

This is deeply troubling, not only because such activities are biblically sinful, but also because such habits are extremely difficult to break. As one of my former students told me, "I hung out with a few guys who started drinking during college. At first I joined in, but pretty soon it got to be almost an everyday sort of thing, and I knew I didn't want that. So, I sort of laid off it for awhile and not long after I got a job and couldn't hang out with them as much. It was a good thing too. I still hang out with them today (eight years later) and a lot of them still drink way too much. It's messed them up pretty good. I sort of feel like I dodged a bullet on that one."

Helping emerging adults as they encounter the ethic of excess is difficult. It seems so simple, "Just say no!" The reality is far more difficult. As with the temptations they face, it seems that open, honest conversations with emerging adults about the ethic of excess might be helpful. In fact, research suggests that emerging adults are more likely to retain the Christian beliefs and practices first developed during adolescence if they have a church or family setting in which they feel they can openly discuss religious matters.[12] It stands to reason that similar frankness could be put into the service of articulating The Ethic of Excess, placing it in a biblical context, and offering support and accountability to avoid it. For emerging adults, such conversations might arise in churches, with parents or among peers. Such a strategy has a biblical basis too. In 1 Corinthians 6:10-13, Paul encourages Christians in Corinth to reign in excesses in sexual conduct, while in 1 Peter 4:3-4, Peter warns Christians not to get caught up in the lifestyle excesses of non-believers.

Christian Higher Education

Because these challenges are real many Christians choose to pursue their studies on Christian college campuses. In the United States there is no shortage of such options as over nine hundred institutions of higher education claim some sort of Christian affiliation. Many emerging adults choose to continue their education on these campuses because they believe that a high-quality education can be attained in an environment more conducive to maintaining faith. In a sense, it is an extension of the principle laid down in Proverbs 22:6, which states, "Train up a child in the way he should go and when he is old he will not depart from it." Such a strategy intuitively makes sense, and on the face of it Christian higher education would seem to offer significant benefits to an emerging adult's Christian faith. Christian colleges immerse emerging adults in a social network of like-minded individuals. We discussed how, even though emerging adults are postponing marriage, a large proportion of them still meet their future spouse during their early emerging adult years. Christian colleges plunge emerging adults into a pool of potential mates who ostensibly share their Christian beliefs.

We have outlined the unique temptations emerging adults face. Christian colleges offer an environment that improves the chances that emerging adults will "be delivered from the Evil One" (Matthew 6:13). Christian colleges typically have in place social and behavioral expectations (i.e. rules) that act as boundaries within which emerging adults can enact their new freedoms. In fact, I used to tell some of my students that the rules at a Christian college were a bit like the Goldilocks fairy tale. Compared to their parent's rules (which were often too hard) and the rules at a secular school (which are always too soft), a Christian college's rules were just right. Christian colleges offer opportunities for accountability, whether through "the rules," mentor relationships with concerned adults, or formal group and social structures. On this last point, I used to frequently tell parents that when a student goes off to college he/she begins to walk a tightrope high above the ground with the very real possibility of falling off and getting hurt. However, Christian colleges offer a safety net beneath the tightrope walker. The students must still walk the tightrope, navigating emerging adulthood and its perils; yet if they make bad choices there are people and structures in place to minimize the detrimental impact.

As good as all of that sounds, is there research to back it up? Yes. In the past decade or so scholars studying Christian higher education have begun to identity a rather wide array of clear cut benefits to that educational path, at least among those schools affiliated with more conservative Protestant faith traditions. One of the most recent and extensive studies examined emerging adults within the Church of Christ faith tradition, a conservative Protestant group among the fifteen largest Christian faiths in the United States. That research project found that 85% of emerging adults in that faith tradition who attended a Christian college remained faithful upon graduation from college.[13] In contrast, less than half of those who attended state-supported schools remained faithful. Another project studying a broader spectrum of conservative Protestant emerging adults also found a relationship between attending a Christian college and retaining Christian faith.[14] In that study the most significant influences occurred outside of the classroom. Additional research details how students attending Christian colleges tend to be more active in their faith.[15] Research even concludes that students attending Christian colleges are less likely to get divorced later in life.[16]

Finally, Christian higher education is not a magic elixir that will insulate emerging adults from all negative outcomes. After working in Christian higher education all of my adult life, I can attest that far too many parents believe that merely sending their children to a Christian college is enough to insure an emerging adult's vibrant Christian faith. Such a belief is idealistic, for a significant amount of research finds that an emerging adult's experiences during childhood and adolescence are far more important in determining their Christian faith than is the Christian college experience.[17]

College and the Erosion of Christian Faith

Another question lurks at the margins of emerging adults and the college years. It is reflected in an experience I had in my first few years of college teaching. On a bright Saturday morning I went to the campus of the Christian college where I taught to participate in a program sponsored by our admissions office in which prospective students and their parents would come to campus, look around, and meet the college faculty and staff. As I sat down to visit with one set of parents, the father looked me in the eye and said, "One thing I want to know up front is this: do you guys teach that liberal stuff? Because I don't hold for that sort of thing and no daughter of mine is going any place where they teach that stuff, understand?" He sat back, folded his arms, and waited for my answer. For a moment I was speechless. What does one say to that? What "liberal stuff" did he have in mind? How do you explain that there's *always* a tension between higher education's pursuit of truth and indoctrination? What right answer was he expecting me to give? What was the wrong answer?

Thinking back on that incident, it is clear to me now that the father was merely giving voice to a common fear of many parents, especially Christian parents. They are afraid that the inevitable exposure to new ideas that accompanies a college education will somehow erode the carefully constructed Christian faith which parents have instilled in their emerging adult children. Does going to college place Christian emerging adults at a greater risk of losing their faith? Does exposure to a wider variety of ideas alter the Christian beliefs an emerging adult holds? These are important questions, and fortunately there is research that speaks to them.

From the 1960s through the 1990s research confirmed what many people suspected: attending college resulted in an increased risk of losing Christian faith. This belief was so strong that some scholars called American colleges "breeding grounds for apostasy."[18] Many reasons were offered for this effect. College students were thrust into an enterprise that emphasized exposure to new ideas in an environment that was often hostile toward religion. Established social support networks were said to be replaced with a new network of more diverse-thinking people. Parents and others who encouraged the maintenance of religious faith were removed from the picture. Plus, the college lifestyle didn't always make it easier to adhere to one's Christian beliefs and practices. Overall, for nearly forty years the common wisdom was that most forms of higher education erode Christian faith.

Today this viewpoint no longer rules. More recent research finds that the current generation of college students' faith is not effected in this way.[19] The most recent and best research available finds that twice as many students report their Christian faith strengthening during their college years as do those claiming that it has waned.[20] Things have changed so much that there is research indicating that those students who do not attend college are at greater risk of losing their faith than those who do attend college.[21]

Why is this? Simply put, the times have changed. There are more Christian organizations and ministries reaching out to college students on campuses across the country. There are more Christians on the faculty and more of a "live and let live" attitude among the students. The worldview of secularism, once promoted and unchallenged on so many college campuses, must now face the same kind of postmodern skepticism as other world-views. When compared with previous generations, today's college students are simply more conventional than their predecessors, especially when it comes to religion. These factors combined paint a very different picture of the role of the college experience in emerging adults' lives.

College as Fire; Students as Snakes

As with most things in life, the relationship between college and Christian faith is a complicated one. As we have seen, there are valid reasons to be concerned about the perils which college and its attendant lifestyle pose to an emerging adults' faith. Yet there is also evidence that it is not college in itself that poses such risks, and that attending college might actually benefit one's Christian faith. So how might one best make sense of all of this?

A few years ago, I was discussing these issues with one of my former students. She was several years removed from college, making her way in life as an emerging adult. As we conversed over burritos at Taco Bell, she was reflecting on her college years and how they influenced her faith. She had attended a Christian college for two years and then transferred to a large state university to complete her degree, so her range of experience was broad. In some ways college was good for her Christian faith while in other ways it was not. Later that evening, as I warmed myself next to the fireplace in my home, I was pondering the spiritual victories and defeats she recounted during that time of her life. As I stared into the fire lost in my thoughts, it hit me: for Christians, college is a lot like fire. Just as fire can be a supreme blessing to our lives offering warmth, a means of cooking and aesthetic beauty, it can also pose a terrible danger. The key is being aware of it, respecting it, and mindfully managing it. I believe that is how Christian emerging adults and those who care about them ought to see college. They need to be keenly aware of the challenges that college will inevitably bring into their lives, and be well prepared to navigate them.

We can look to Jesus' words in Matthew 10 for guidance. Matthew recalls how Jesus sent his disciples out into the world on their own for the first time. He warned them what to expect once they are immersed as his ambassadors in an environment removed from the immediate presence of the Master. He said, "I am sending you out like sheep among wolves. Therefore, be as shrewd as snakes and innocent as doves." Many emerging adults have gotten down the part about being innocent as doves. They blithely go off to college focused on the educational opportunities and the exhilarating life experiences that accompany it. They do not realize they are playing with fire. They don't respect the speed with which temptations can come upon them. They don't realize the slow drift their Christian faith can experience. They don't clearly see the subtle compromises they easily make to their beliefs and practice. Too few emerging adults are shrewd like snakes. The shrewd ones recognize the blessings that the college experience can bring and know how to reap them while avoiding the ever-present traps. They spend time at church and in the library. They have friends in biology and in Bible class. They enjoy their new freedoms within sensible boundaries. They seek out new friends and new Christian mentors. Recognizing that while they are in college they are "aliens and strangers in the world" (1 Peter 2:11), they zealously guard their Christian faith (1 Corinthians 16:13).

College can be a pivotal season of life for the Christian emerging adult. In many ways it is the framework upon which an adult's later life is built. Emerging adults owe it to themselves and we owe it to them to consider the college experience in a clear-headed, proactive manner.

Discussion Questions

1. How can emerging adults best be prepared to resist the detrimental explorations and excesses of college?

2. Is the chapter's case for Christian higher education persuasive to you? Why don't more parents and emerging adults opt for that choice?

3. What about those emerging adults who do not go to college? How is their emerging adult experience different?

Parenting
Emerging Adults

The Christian parents of two emerging adult children sat at their kitchen table worriedly discussing the children's latest developments. One was wandering in the wilderness of emerging adulthood, not attending church and keeping God at arm's distance. The child had not "gone off the deep end," yet clearly spiritual things had fallen far down the list of life's priorities. As mom and dad talked over a cup of coffee, you could see the anxiety on their faces and hear the concern in their voices. They had been stellar parents raising their kids in healthy Christian homes, and so their child's plight puzzled them. They seemed paralyzed as to what to do about it. At first they argued, then they pleaded, then they dropped it, then they asked some friends to try their hand at it. As their coffee grew colder that afternoon, they felt as if they were at a dead end, unsure of what to do next. What their child ought to do was so obvious to them, yet they felt powerless to get their child to see it that way. They had prayed fervently about their child's situation and they wanted so badly to trust in the Lord to work things out, but it had been months now and things were not getting better. If anything, they sensed that things might be getting worse. Soon they simply sat in silence as the afternoon sun streamed through their kitchen window.

It's fine to talk about emerging adults and their Christian faith, but let's not forget the parents. They too must navigate the treacherous waters of emerging adulthood, but as observers rather than as direct participants. As one of my friends currently parenting a college student told me, "These years are just as hard on me as it is on my child but in a completely different way." Another observed, "There are plenty of manuals on how to raise young kids but where's the one on how to parent a twenty-six year-old?" One of my students' parents confided to me during new student orientation: "This is our third child in college. You would think we had a handle on parenting kids this age, but we haven't got a clue. Sometimes, I think it's harder than when they were little." I still vividly remember facilitating a meeting during my college's new student orientation program where the students' parents are invited to meet one another and the college staff. A portion of that program featured a time for parents to introduce themselves and say something about their newly dropped-off college students. One intrepid husband introduced himself and his wife and proudly said, "We're thrilled to be here today dropping off the last child to leave the nest because after today our job as parents is done." Everyone in the room laughed at him. And, we were not laughing *with* him; we were laughing *at* him because we knew how mistaken he was! (By the way, when I bumped into him three years later he had come to a different conclusion.)

Parenting emerging adults is challenging. Though it can be filled with pride and joy, it can also be riddled with disappointment and heartache. And so, our attention now turns to addressing some of these challenges.

"I Can Do It Myself"

A long-time family friend of mine has a three year-old child whose favorite phrase right now is, "I can do it myself!" Whether it is putting on her shoes or pouring milk into a cup, she is absolutely convinced that since she is now a big girl she does not need her parents' help to complete such tasks. After all, in her eyes she's not a kid anymore; she's sufficiently grown to where she is autonomous and independent. The phrase "I can do it myself" strikes at the heart of the child's relationship with her parents. It signals a change from how things used to be when she recognized that she didn't know how to put on her shoes or couldn't manage the milk jug on her own. It announces that, in light of her newly acquired growth and knowledge, her parents must play a new role of observer of her self-directed actions. In many ways, emerging adulthood reflects an identical set of circumstances. Just as a three-year old and her parent must adjust to the child's growth by renegotiating each other's roles, so too must an emerging adult and his/her parent. Parents and children are still connected, but in a new way that both of them must figure out. As one researcher observed, the challenges for emerging adults and their parents revolve around "the psychological component of establishing self as a separate, yet connected individual and questions such as 'When is the appropriate time for emerging adults to make their own decisions based on their own beliefs and values?'"[1]

One challenge, then, is that parents must acknowledge their child as an emerging adult and accept what that implies for themselves as parents. Research finds that such recognition facilitates a child's healthy transition to adulthood; when it is absent the child's development is impaired.[2] In biblical times, this was often accomplished when a father pronounced a blessing on his child (e.g. Genesis 27:27-29). In American culture today, there really isn't anything equivalent to that. So parents often struggle to know when and how to recognize their children as emerging adults.

Many of my students over the years have told me stories of how, when they went home between college terms, their parents would speak to them and treat them as if they were still adolescents. This was difficult for them, especially if they had been living on their own some distance away from home. One of my current students reflected the same struggle when she recently told me, "Every time I go home my parents treat me like I'm the same person I was when I went off to college. They expect me to live by the same rules I had when I was in high school. They just don't get that I'm in college now." When I asked a recent college graduate about this, he rolled his eyes and said, "Even now when I go home to visit, my parents act like nothing has changed. I don't think they really see me as an adult." Another of my former students related to me that every time she visited home in the years immediately after her graduation from college her parents acted as if nothing had changed in her life. She was still expected to do the same household chores as when she was living at home. She was still expected to notify her parents when she left the house as to where she was going, who she would be with, and when she might return. And she is not alone. A surprising number of my former students report similar situations.

For some parents, it is hard to see their children as anything but children, even when they physically look like adults and are clearly doing adult things such as moving away and living on their own. It's as if in the parent's mind the child is frozen in an earlier time of life when perhaps the parenting was easiest or the memories were the best. This sort of thinking makes it extremely difficult to parent during the emerging adult years, creating interpersonal conflict between parents and children and further complicating an emerging adult's transition to adulthood.

And yet, parents must recognize their emerging adult children for what they have become: emerging *adults*. Psychologist William Aquilino notes that parents seeing their children as adults and children seeing their parents as people rather than simply as parents is "one of the key developmental tasks of emerging adulthood that sets the stage for later care-giving and mutual support as parents move from midlife to old age and their offspring into middle adulthood."[3] If parents do not do so, they run the risk of needlessly complicating and delaying their children's transition to full adulthood. In his book, *Emptying the Nest: Launching Your Young Adult toward Success and Self-Reliance*, psychologist Brad Sachs uses his experiences counseling parents and emerging adults to place families into categories based on the extent to which they help or hinder emerging adults in the transition to full adulthood. Those in the most unhelpful category are the ones who, among other things, refuse to explicitly recognize the adult dimension of their emerging adult children. He goes on to note that the emerging adults parented in this manner have the most difficult time during emerging adulthood.[4]

I have always been stuck by a statement that John the Baptist made to his disciples. Speaking of his ministry in light of Jesus' emerging ministry, he is recorded as saying, "Jesus must become greater; I must become less" (John 3:30). With those words, John acknowledged Jesus' superiority to himself, but he recognized something else too—that his own role would soon diminish. John the Baptist was a fine opening act, but when the headliner appears (Jesus) it is time for the opening act to leave the stage. During the childhood and teenage years parents have the stage to themselves as the opening act. But during emerging adulthood the headliners appear and it is time for the opening act to step aside. Of course, human nature wants to remain the headliner, and so many opening acts find it hard to take their bows and exit. Yet this is precisely what John the Baptist did. He models for parents an attitude of graciousness and acceptance towards the time-limited nature of the roles we play. Ecclesiastes 3:1 also reminds us of this when it notes, "There is a time for everything and a season for every activity under heaven."

"Is there a book for this?"

I was eating lunch with a friend not long ago and we were discussing our kids. I explained to him the latest parenting challenges related to teaching my teenagers how to drive. He was relating to me his struggles to parent an emerging adult child living far away and edging closer to an engagement to someone whom the parents had never met and knew little about. We both laughed ruefully and observed that in some ways it was easier for us when our kids were younger and all we had to do was insure that they were clothed, fed, and had their diapers changed. That was relatively easy; we understood and knew how to do that. Then, my friend noted that the long-distance parenting of an emerging adult is infinitely more complicated and said to me, "Is there a book for this?"

Another challenge is that most parents are uncertain as to how to parent emerging adults. This, in turn, leads to a great deal of and apprehension on a parent's part, and it is easy to see why: parents are caught amidst conflicting concerns. They know that now their parenting needs to change, yet they are not sure what that ought to look like. Though successful parents through the teenage years, some of what made them so are no longer in place and parents often don't know what to do when they are absent. They have a genuine desire to continue to play an important role in the children's life, but their emerging adult child envisions a diminishing role. Parents seem caught between knowing that their role must shrink and maintaining some active parental role. When people feel pulled in opposite directions and uncertainty rises, they tend to revert back to the familiar. In this case, it means a return to the "default setting" of whatever role was played during the previous stage of the child's life.

Parents of emerging adults hate to admit to their emerging adult children that they often feel as if they do not know how to parent them. Parents are used to being in an authoritative, all-knowing position in relation to their children. That is, there is a clear undercurrent to parenting that suggests to the school-aged or teenage child, "I'm the parent. I am older and wiser than you. Therefore, I know how to parent you." And so, during their children's at-home years there's not much talk between parents and children of how parents ought to parent (other than the child's complaints about the fairness or effectiveness of such parenting!). As one frustrated parent of two teenagers recently told her daughters, "I'm your mother and this is not a democracy." This is appropriate when kids are younger, for during those years they are not mature enough to participate as partners in their parenting. Yet as maturity and life experiences rise during emerging adulthood, children become more viable partners in the parenting process. The gap in authority and experiences begins to shrink considerably. This opens up the possibility that parents can more readily talk to their children about parenting and with greater transparency open a dialogue about the struggles they face in renegotiating parent-child roles.

Following the Script

When my children were still infants, I remember often standing over their cribs holding their tiny hands to sooth them as they fell asleep. I would often look down into their crib and wonder what they would be like when they grew up and what course their life would take. I wondered who they would marry, and when they would marry. I mused about where they might go to college, and what they might study there. I imagined the jobs they might attain and the path of their careers. In my mind, I had it all figured out. My kids would grow up in the suburbs of a large city, and be deeply involved in our local church. They would get good grades in school and participate in many extracurricular activities, especially basketball. They would go off to a Christian college in another state and major in something that clearly leads to a good job and bright career. While in school, they will meet a strong Christian with whom they fall in love, and marry when well established financially.

As you can see, I have definite ideas about how my kids life ought to be—the choices they ought to make and the path they ought to follow. Evidently I am not the only one who has these notions. A family friend of mine relates the story of how when her daughter was still an infant, she would wait until she was asleep and then bend down to her daughter's ear and whisper into it, "Good girls don't get married until after graduate school!"

Psychologist Joan Atwood explains that parents have very specific ideas in mind for their children as to which paths they will follow as their lives unfold. She calls these "family scripts," and she believes that they are powerful influences on parents and children's interactions with one another.[5] Family scripts function for children much as a script does for an actor in a play, guiding one's actions, indicating which choices are to be made, where one is to be, and how one is to look. However, unlike the script an actor holds in his hand, family scripts are usually less conspicuous and tangible. Sometimes they reside only in a parent's mind and are not made clear, as when a father assumes that his son will be outgoing like he is and therefore be popular in school and run for student council. At other times, family scripts are explicitly articulated, as when a mother tells her child that she must take piano lessons because that's what she did as a child and she benefited greatly from them. And, of course, just as an actor can choose to

follow or deviate from the script, so too children can "improvise" or "go off
script." As I write this, my kids are in high school, one a junior and one a
freshman. Both have not followed the script that I had in my head for them
to follow. I thought they would play basketball; neither does. I thought they
would both be staunch leaders deeply involved in the church youth group,
attending every activity and seizing leadership roles at every turn; instead
both are involved but not in the ways that I imagined.

Family scripts are good and useful things, proving themselves invaluable in ordering expectations and behaviors. In fact, one might say that the
Bible gives some examples of family scripts. For instance, Genesis 24:3-4
describes how Abraham had it in is head that his son Isaac would not marry
a Canaanite woman but would instead be married to someone from his own
clan. And 1 Samuel 1:11 shows Hannah making an explicit promise to God
what her son will be if God were to bless her with a son.

The role of scripts becomes especially important during emerging
adulthood. With their new freedom to choose the course of their lives,
emerging adults enter the phase in life when children are most likely to
deviate from the script their parents have envisioned for them. As you might
imagine, when emerging adults don't follow the script, there's tension and
conflict. Indeed, research finds that one of the most common sources of
conflict between parents and their emerging adult children occurs when
the family script is not followed.[6]

One couple I know experienced significant conflict with their emerging adult daughter because she chose to drop out of college after a year in
order to go to a program leading to a career as a foreign missionary. They
said, "We always thought she would go to college. We always talked about
that and saved our money to help her with that. Now she decides to do
this. We have no problem with being a missionary. It's just not at all what
we expected." Another couple I know is greatly concerned that their single
daughter has not yet shown any interest in getting married. Many years out
of college, she is still unattached and not looking. And it's not a case that
they desire grandchildren. It's that in their mind they expected her to be

married by now because, as one of the parents told me, "That's just what Christian girls do."

When emerging adult children don't follow the script, they tend to see it as simply a normal function of making choices for themselves. It's as if they say, "I suppose my parents thought I would choose path X but I have chosen path Y because it works out better for me. It's just my choice, that's all." In other words, to emerging adults it's no big deal. But for their parents it often *is* a big deal. In their eyes, when an emerging adult deviates from the family script he/she is not only rejecting whatever paths were not chosen, but much more. The parents often feel as if *they* are rejected too. Deviating from the script implicitly calls into question the parent's judgment as to what is best for an emerging adult. Deviating from the script is fundamentally an assertion of the emerging adult's power over his/her own life, and thus it acts to reaffirm that the parent's influence is waning.

How ought parents to deal with inevitable deviations from the family script? I believe that parents ought to re-frame such deviations. In my communication classes I teach the concept of framing, which is the idea that when faced with the need to offer some interpretation of an event or a decision we consciously choose one interpretation over another—usually an interpretation that suits our own, larger agenda. As mentioned above, emerging adults frame their choice to deviate from the family script as an enactment of their new-found freedom, while their parents often frame the exact same choice as a rejection of their proffered wisdom. Notice that even the words used to describe the choices ("rejection" as opposed to "deviation") hint at the differing frames invoked to interpret the same choice. Experience tells us that when frames conflict it is usually quite hard to convince others to accept our frame, and so it is sometimes profitable to derive an alternative frame from the two initially offered.

In the case of emerging adults deviating from the family script, I suggest that parents re-frame such choices in two ways. First, parents can see the deviations from the script as opportunities to practice godliness. For example, many parents get frustrated when the script is not followed. What a marvelous opportunity to practice the patience that the Bible in Ephesians 4:2 calls Christians to develop! Also, deviations from the script all too often lead to intense conflicts, which offer opportunities to control anger (James 1:19-20) and practice unselfishness (Philippians 4:3-4). Second, parents can re-frame deviations from the script as opportunities to give gifts to their emerging adult children. Usually, we think of gift-giving as bestowing some tangible item on a special occasion. However, it is also possible to conceive of gifts as non-tangible things given in the course of everyday interactions. For example, since the Bible calls us to be self-controlled (1 Thessalonians 5:6-8), we can give our spouses that gift whenever we check our desires to lose our tempers or lash out with a harsh remark. So parents might re-frame their emerging adult child's deviation from the family script as an opportunity to give them the gift of encouragement (Hebrews 10:25) by not responding in a negative, unsupportive manner. Parents can choose to respond to deviations from the Family Script in either a self-focused ("*My script has been rejected!*") or an other-focused manner ("I can place God's or my child's interests above my own.").

Relating as Equals

From as early as I can remember until the present, I have always referred to my mother as "Mom." I cannot ever recall using her first name when in conversation with her. Like most American children, I use my parent's role title (mom) rather than her first name (Vivia) when speaking with her. So you can imagine my surprise when I tagged along with my college roommate one weekend to visit his parents. As we walked in the door, he hugged his mother and sweetly said, "Hi, Joan." I was dumbfounded! It absolutely blew my mind that he would call her by her first name. Later, I timidly asked if Joan were his stepmother, thinking that perhaps she might be and that my roommate was therefore uncomfortable bestowing the title of "mom" on her. "No, she's my biological mother," replied my roommate. "Then why do you call her Joan?'" I asked. My roommate shrugged and said, "Because that's her name."

In my communication classes, I explain that power is a dynamic that operates in the background of most communicative interactions. For example, at the college where I teach, the students are in the habit of calling the teachers "Dr. Simmons" or "Professor Simmons." By using such honorific titles they are not only communicating respect for the faculty, they are also subtly reinforcing the reality that the faulty have more power than they do, that ours is an unequal relationship. However, I have always encouraged my students to abandon the "Dr. Simmons" and "Professor Simmons" and simply call me "Brian." I do this because of my teaching philosophy that students learn better when the power gap between the student and the teacher is diminished, and one way to do this is to permit students to call me "Brian." In a sense, by encouraging them to call me "Brian" I am trying to level out a typically unequal relationship and make it more equal.

Similarly, when their children get to be emerging adults, parents tend to relate to them differently than they did when they were adolescents—they begin to relate to them more as equals. As one researcher noted,

> Although emerging adults are more independent than they were as adolescents, in some ways they become closer to parents. The hierarchy of parent as authority figure, child as dependent and subordinate, fades away. What remains, in most cases, is the mutual affection and attachment they have for one another on the basis of many years of shared experiences. They learn to see each other as persons, as individuals, rather than being defined strictly by their roles as parent and child. They talk about a wider range of subjects than they did before and they do so more openly, more as friends.[7]

Though the transition to this new way of relating is often uneven and difficult, it is typically welcomed. Research finds that most parents look favorably on this new form of relationship, especially mothers.[8] Such sentiment is well captured by a pendant I saw recently worn by the mother of an emerging adult child. It was inscribed with the words, "Always my daughter, now too my friend." Furthermore, emerging adults see the relationship in more positive terms too. One study found that emerging adults who move an hour or more drive away from home report feeling closer to their parents and valuing their opinions more.[9] Another study found that as adolescents transition into emerging adults the frequency and severity of conflict with their parents decreases.[10]

The improving relationship between emerging adults and their parents plays a crucial role in the maintenance of an emerging adult's Christian faith. A substantial amount of research concludes that parents are the most significant influence on a teenager's Christian faith, even more so than teenage peers.[11] Though diminished somewhat, this influence continues into emerging adulthood. One study found that over 90% of emerging adults describe themselves as holding similar Christian beliefs as their parents.[12] The same study found that emerging adults and parents tend to get along better when their religious beliefs are in line with one another. Too many parents seem to be under the impression that they have little influence over their child's Christian faith once they enter emerging adulthood. This is simply not the case. Emerging adults tend to still give great weight to their parent's authority and, in fact, continue to be effected by previous parental religious influences that occurred during adolescence.

Yet even though emerging adults relate to their parents *more* as equals and generally see an improved relationship, they are never 100% equals. This is where the problems creep in, especially concerning matters of Christian faith. Emerging adults are usually empowered by the transition to a more equal relationship with their parents and assume that this new found equality will carry with it a mutual respect for the choices that the emerging adult might make. For example, one of my former students related to me that he chose to leave the faith tradition in which he was raised and affiliate with another one. He knew that his parents would not be pleased, but he assumed that, since he and his parents were more equal in their relationship, they would agree to disagree. Hence, he was mystified and annoyed when his parents reacted harshly to his decision and did not get on board with it.

In his eyes, they were being inconsistent and not treating him as an equal. Meanwhile, I can imagine exactly what his parents were thinking: "Yes, our son is more equal with us than he once was, but that doesn't mean we are going to stop being parents, especially when it comes to important matters of Christian faith."

My former student's experience makes clear that parents struggle to balance two competing interests: treating their emerging adult children as equals and being faithful to their role as parents. Communication researcher Leslie Baxter refers to such competing interests as "dialectics" to get at the fact that two valued concerns are in tension.[13] Managing the dialectics is difficult partly because it operates in the background of parent-child relationships until popping up in different forms. This might be illustrated in a conflict between parents and their daughter's decision to purchase an expensive new car. The parents feel obligated *as parents* to give the child sound financial advice, however the daughter is offended because in doing so the parents are not treating her *as an equal* who is competent to make her own decisions about financial matters.

One of the skills to be gained in parenting emerging adult children is managing dialectical tension; but the complexity of these tensions makes it impossible to offer universal guidelines. Managing such dialectical tensions is nothing new to Christians, for the New Testament frequently calls them to manage the tension between competing concerns. For example, Jesus can be seen encouraging his followers not to judge people (Matthew 7:1-2), but also not ignoring blatantly sinful behavior (John 8:11, Matthew 23:13-15). Jesus sends his disciples out telling them to spread the gospel (Matthew 10:5-8), but at times to give up on some who reject it (10:11-16). Paul preaches a message of forgiveness (2 Corinthians 2:7-10) as well as a message recommending that some be expelled from Christian fellowship (5:1-5). Christian parents of emerging adult children can work to transfer their skills in managing the dialectical tensions of the Christian life to managing them in their parenting. If nothing else, it always helps to pray for wisdom (James 2:5).

Connection and Control

A related dialectical dynamic poses an additional challenge to the parents of emerging adult children: the tension between connection and control. In her book, *I Only Say This Because I Love You: How the Way We Talk Can Make or Break Family Relationships Throughout Our Lives*, communication researcher Deborah Tannen explains that parents' communication with their emerging adult children is driven by two often conflicting desires: the desire to feel close to their child (connection) and the desire to impose their wishes on their child (control). Good parents strive to satisfy both desires, yet doing so is often misinterpreted. As Tannen says, "What looks to be a control maneuver could just as well be a connection maneuver—or both at once."[14]

Consider this example. An emerging adult is visiting his parents for the weekend and mentions that he has recently applied for a new credit card so he can accumulate frequent flyer miles. His father asks how many credit cards he has, to which he responds, "Five." His parent admonishes him to cut up all but one, warning him of the perils of high credit card debt. This triggers a hostile response from the son, who counters that he's perfectly capable of managing his own money. And besides, he is financially independent anyway, so it's really none of their business. An argument ensues leaving both grumpy for the remainder of his weekend visit.

In this scenario, the father was trying to do what he's always done for the child—offer wise perspective and guidance (which in Tannen's language might be termed a smattering of connection mixed in with an obvious play for control). But the emerging adult son sees the conversation as an inappropriate infringement on his freedom and an indication that he's not the adult he claims to be (or, in Tannen's language, too much control).

It seems to me that the competing dynamics of connection and control are likely to be especially prevalent when it comes to matters of Christian faith. First, the New Testament seems to recognize the interplay of connection and control. Ephesians 6:4 exhorts fathers not to exasperate their children but instead to "bring them up in the training and admonition of the

Lord." Exasperation often arises when parents have not adequately provided or communicated connection or when they have mishandled attempts to control their children. Second, since Christian parents believe it is so important for their emerging adult children to have a healthy Christian faith, they are likely to try to extend the influence they had over their adolescent children into the later years. Rarely will the next generation's religious beliefs and practices line up 100% with those of their parents. Plus, we noted previously that today's emerging adults are especially prone to see religious belief and practice differently than did previous generations. These two factors alone nearly guarantee that there will be some disparity of belief and practice between Christian parents and their emerging adult children. As a result, parents will be motivated to exert influence (control) over their emerging adult children to close this gap.

Failure to Launch

In 2006, Paramount Pictures released the film *Failure to Launch* in which an emerging adult with no job and little motivation in life continues to live with his parents. Because they want to support their son, the parents are at first receptive to this arrangement. But as time goes on, they feel that it is time for their son to "launch into the world," and the film centers on their efforts to help him to do that. The film's title implies that "launching" is what is supposed to happen and that when it doesn't something is wrong. Indeed, if you ask most American parents what their goals are in raising children, most will tell you that, among other things, they want them to be independent. Emerging adults heartily agree, for in their eyes they do not become full adults until they accept responsibility for themselves, make independent decisions, and achieve financial independence from their parents.[15]

Parents and their children have come to expect that a certain timeline will be followed: children will live at home until they graduate from high school, after which they will launch out on their own to attend college, get a job, move into their own residence, join the military, travel abroad, or something like that. Regardless of what comes next after they leave home, emerging adults are expected to "launch," and parents are expected to prepare them. But "launching" is different for today's emerging adults, as more and more emerging adults are leaving home only to return. In the 1920s, only about one in five Americans returned home after they initially left. Today research finds that nearly half of all emerging adults will move back in with their parents for an extended period of time (not counting summers home from college).[16] Furthermore, about a quarter of emerging adults do not leave home for the first time until age twenty-two or later.[17] Fifty years ago this would have seemed odd. It might even have been looked at as a failure on the parents' part. Yet research indicates that many parents understand that today's economy requires a longer period at home in order to properly "launch."[18]

Yet parents do worry. In fact, though they hate to admit it, parents fear that how their emerging child turns out is a highly visible statement about their success as parents. An old proverb says, "The apple doesn't fall far from the tree."And so, many parents sense a negative stigma attached to them when their emerging adult children "fail to launch." They worry that if the family script isn't followed then others will look down on their parenting skills. Christian parents often feel that if their children change faith traditions or abandon their faith then others at church will question the parenting during the years the child was still at home. Because the Bible places a heavy responsibility on parents to raise their children in the ways of the Lord (Deuteronomy 6:1-4), this expectation is likely to be especially potent for Christian parents. One parent candidly admitted to me that she was embarrassed to tell her friends that her daughter was no longer worshipping in the faith tradition in which she was raised. She said, "Maybe it's in my head, but I feel as if they're judging me as a bad parent." Another parent told me that, while he didn't feel that others looked down on them as parents, his spouse did feel that way: "She won't admit it, but I know she feels that way; and it's hard on her."

Emerging adults tend not to realize that their life choices after high school reflect on their parents. To the contrary, most emerging adults I have talked to are surprised to learn about the links between their choices and their parent's reputation. They're perplexed to hear that their parents think this way because, to the emerging adult awash in new freedom and independence, their choices are exactly that—*their choices*. As one told me, "They ought to butt out!" Another emerging adult who left the Christian faith wrote to me, saying, "It's ludicrous to say that my decision to stop believing in God somehow reflects on my parents. They could not have done anything differently that would have led me to a different decision." However, one of my former students confessed to me that she was aware that her parents felt as if others were judging them, and she admitted that it bothers her. "It [stinks] that my mom and dad feel that way. I never intended that and people who think that way are messed up. But, yeah, it's hard on me. I mean, I'm not going to change my life because of it or anything. It just [stinks]."

Some Specific Suggestions for Parents

What advice can be given to parents of emerging adults? First, talk openly and honestly to your emerging adult children about your struggles in parenting them. One thing I frequently say to students in my communication courses is that relationships work more smoothly if people talk explicitly about what is really going on rather than dancing around it. One of my standard phrases is, "Why can't anybody be honest with anybody?" The Bible calls it "Speaking the truth in love" (Ephesians 4:15) and much research suggests that such an approach makes for better relationships.[19]

In the spirit of starting profitable conversations, parents would do well to explicitly identify and talk about their parenting struggles. They might say, "I am not certain how to parent you now that you're in college" or, "I want to offer my opinions to you but I know that I cannot tell you what to do like I used to do, so help me understand how I can express my opinions without you thinking that I am running your life." One set of parents I know tried this. They had been in constant conflict with their emerging adult college student ever since she had returned home for the summer in between academic terms. Finally, after one particularly frustrating argument, her mother said to her in exasperation, "I just don't know what to do for you right now! I feel as if everything I used to know about parenting is useless now. Nothing seems to work for me and all we ever do is fight, and I don't want that. I am tired of it. Please, tell me what you want from me. Tell me how I can fit into your life and still be a parent." Her daughter was stunned into silence by her mother's baldly honest vulnerability, and it triggered a reciprocal response from her daughter. She admitted that she didn't know what she wanted from her mother, and that she too was trying to figure out how to be the adult child of a parent who still desired to be involved in her life. That unexpected dose of honesty from both parties broke a logjam in their relationship and paved the way for a heartfelt discussion and a better relationship.

Second, regardless of what develops in an emerging adult's life, continue to communicate love and concern. Though this would seem obvious, I am continually amazed at the number of parents who struggle with this. One set of parents told me that after their son graduated from college he left their faith tradition for another one. Alarmed, his parents told him in no uncertain terms that they vehemently disagreed with his decision and that he was no longer welcome in their home until he "repented" and returned to the faith tradition of his youth. Another set of parents adopted the same approach when their daughter moved away from home and moved in with her boyfriend. Her father refused to speak with her, leaving her mother feeling caught between her husband and her daughter. Both families offered me the same explanation: "We want our child to know how serious this is to us and we don't want her to think we approve of what she are doing."

Such sentiment reflects the quandary that faces many parents—how to support the emerging adult child without endorsing what they do. While there is a biblical basis for cutting off habitual interactions with Christians *in extreme situations* (1 Corinthians 5:1-11), such an action ought to be a last resort. Well prior to such drastic measures parents would do well to adopt a strategy that communicates the twin messages, "We love you and are concerned about you, but we are in deep disagreement with your choice."

These seem to be the messages that Jesus communicated to the Samaritan woman he met by the well (John 4:7-26) and to the adulterous woman brought before him (John 8:1-11). These also seem to be the messages Paul communicates to the Corinthians (2 Corinthians 2:5-11). In addition to the Bible's divine wisdom, recent research finds that messages of love and concern coupled with clear disagreement over someone's choices create the best environment for bringing wayward Christians back to the faith.[20]

There is another reason why parents ought to be careful about what messages they send to their emerging adult children. In my communication courses, I frequently talk about the notion of "allies and enemies." These terms refer to people's tendency to place those around them into categories according to whether they perceive them as on their side (allies) or as against them (enemies). For example, over the years it was not uncommon for students to announce to me that they were engaged to be married. In many cases, I felt that the engagement had come too quickly, or that the fiancé was a bad choice, or that the engagement was merely a way to escape a bad situation at home. Early in my teaching career, I learned that if I immediately and strongly expressed my disagreement with the choice that my student would mentally place me in the category of enemy and would avoid talking with me about the subject again. As a result, I would lose my avenue of influence. As time went on, I learned to react less critically to the initial announcement of an engagement with which I had reservations because I found that in doing so, I was placed into the category of ally, thus preserving my avenue of influence. I discovered that students gave my words greater credibility. I believe that parents of emerging adults would be wise to adopt a similar approach.

Finally, parents should genuinely make their peace with the reality that their emerging adult's Christian faith will likely not look exactly like what they thought or hoped it would be. Again, this seems obvious, yet many parents seem to struggle with it. I know parents who are deeply disappointed with their emerging adult children because they only attend worship services on Sunday morning and not mid-week services. I know other parents who grieve for their child's soul because she left one congregation within a specific conservative Protestant faith tradition to attend another congregation *within the same conservative Protestant faith tradition*. I know of a parent whose emerging adult child attends church faithfully and is actively involved in the faith tradition in which she was raised, but holds very different beliefs about baptism, the role of women in public worship, and homosexuality. To the parent, such beliefs are deviant and wrong, and have been the source of tremendous angst in the parent's life.

We must tread carefully when discussing this sort of thing because there is the legitimate, biblical statement that some things are true and some things are false. As Christians, emerging adult parents rightfully desire to stand for truth (e.g. 1 Peter 2:1-3, 1 Timothy 4:1-3). But there are also human traditions (e.g. Colossians 2:8, Matthew 23:1-22) and disputable matters (Romans 14:1). Still, the Bible also speaks of the need to attain wisdom and discernment (Proverbs 3:13, 4:7, 16:21). I believe that parents need to pray for the wisdom (James 1:5) to know how to respond to the inevitable differences between a parent's vision of their emerging adult child's Christian faith and what actually comes to pass. Doing so makes it more likely that a parent will be able to accurately discern the vital from the less important and the non-negotiable from the optional.

DISCUSSION QUESTIONS

1. If you are the parent of an emerging adult consider this: what's the hardest part of parenting an emerging adult?

2. Is it possible for parents and emerging adults to have meaningful dialogue about parenting during these years? What might such dialogue look like?

3. In what ways have you seen Deborah Tannen's connection and control notion?

4. To what extent have you experienced feelings that how your emerging adult children turn out reflects on your parenting?

5. What family scripts do you envision for your children? Are they being followed?

Epilogue

This book began with the story of a former student of mine sharing her frustrations as an emerging adult. The day she and I spoke, she was wandering in the wilderness, her Christian faith suffocating beneath the pressures of emerging adulthood. That was nearly ten years ago. Today, she is married to a godly man who shares her interest in mission work and together they are faithful and active members of a vibrant church. She made it out of the wilderness and onto clear paths.

Yet for every one like her there are others who remain mired in the wilderness. Theirs is not a wilderness of darkness and tall, dense undergrowth. It is a wilderness where things might seem as if they are not that bad; physically, emotionally, and socially they might even be thriving. But spiritually they are hollow. We all know someone in that wilderness. I hope this book provides the knowledge and encouragement to rescue those who remain in the wilderness. Psalm 136:16 speaks of God leading his people Israel through the wilderness. He did so then and he can do so now.

Endnotes

Introduction

1   Howard Brinton, *Quaker Journals: Varieties of Religious Experiences among Friends* (Wallingford, PA.: Pendle Hill Publications, 1972).

Chapter One

1   Jeffrey Jensen Arnett, "Emerging Adulthood: Understanding the New Way of Coming of Age," in *Emerging Adults in America: Coming of age in the 21st Century*, ed. Jeffrey Jensen Arnett and Jennifer Lynn Tanner (New York: American Psychological Association, 2006), 4.
2   Ibid., 4.
3   Ibid., 6.
4   Ibid.
5   Alex Williams, "The New Math on Campus." *New York Times*, February 5, 2010, http://www.nytimes.com/2010/02/07/fashion/07campus.html.
6   Arnett, "Emerging Adulthood: Understanding the New Way of Coming of Age," 7.
7   Social Security Administration, http://www.ssa.gov/OACT/STATS/table4c6.html.
8   Frank Furstenburg, Jr., Sheela Kennedy, Vonnie McCloyd, Ruben Rumbaut, and & Richard Settersten, Jr., "Between Adolescence and Adulthood: Expectations about the Timing of Adulthood," in *Network Transitions to Adulthood and Public Policy Working Papers* (Philadelphia, PA: University of Pennsylvania, 2003), 34.
9   Robert Wuthnow, *After the Baby Boomers: How Twenty- and Thirty-Somethings are Shaping the Future of American Religion* (Princeton, NJ: Princeton University Press, 2007), 13.
10   Jeffrey Jensen Arnett, *Emerging Adulthood: The Winding Road from the Late Teens through the Twenties* (New York: Oxford University Press, 2004), 6.
11   Arnett, "Emerging Adulthood: Understanding the New Way of Coming of Age," 209.
12   Arnett, *Emerging Adulthood: The Winding Road from the Late Teens through the Twenties*, 222-223.
13   Sharon Parks, *The Critical Years: The Young Adult Search for a Faith to Live By* (San Francisco: Harper and Row, 1986), 96.
14   Christian Smith, *Souls in Transition: The Religious and Spiritual Lives of Emerging Adults* (New York: Oxford University Press, 2009), 111.
15   Arnett, "Emerging Adulthood: Understanding the New Way of Coming of Age," 8.
16   Ibid., 9.
17   Ibid.
18   Ibid., 10.
19   Ibid., 13.
20   Ibid.

Chapter Two

1   Erik Erickson, *Adulthood* (New York: Norton, 1978), 125.
2   William Perry, *Intellectual and Ethical Development in the College Years: A Scheme* (New York: Holt, Rhinehart & Winston, 1968).
3   Sharon Parks, "Young Adult Faith Development: Teaching in the Context of Theological Education," in Jeff Astley and Leslie J. Francis, eds., *Christian Perspectives on Faith Development* (Grand Rapids, MI: Eerdmans, 1992).
4   Ibid., 202.

5   Vonnie Gillespie, *Experience of Faith* (Birmingham, AL: Religious Education Press, 1988), 178.
6   Ibid., 181.
7   Brian Simmons, *Falling Away: Why Christians Lose Their Faith and What Can Be Done about It* (Abilene, TX: Leafwood Publishers, 2008).
8   Ibid., 72.

Chapter Three

1   Robert Wuthnow, *After the Baby Boomers: How Twenty- and Thirty-Somethings Are Shaping the Future of American Religion* (Princeton, NJ: Princeton University Press), 15.
2   Ibid., 15.
3   Ibid., 100.
4   Christian Smith. *Souls in Transition: The Religious and Spiritual Lives of Emerging Adults* (New York: Oxford University Press), 134.
5   Ibid., 136.
6   Christian Smith, *Soul Searching: The Religious and Spiritual Lives of American Teenagers* (New York: Oxford University Press, 2005), 82.
7   Smith, *Souls in Transition*, 157.
8   Jeffrey Arnett, *Emerging Adulthood: The Long and Winding Road from the Late Teens through the Twenties* (New York: Oxford University Press, 2004), 172.
9   Wuthnow, *After the Baby Boomers*, 121.
10   Nancy Ammerman, "Golden Rule Christianity: Lived Religion in the American Mainstream," in *Lived Religion in the American Mainstream: Toward a History of Practice*, edited by David D. Hall (Princeton, NJ: Princeton University Press, 1997), 196-216.
11   Smith, *Souls in Transition*, 146.
12   Wuthnow, *After the Baby Boomers*, 121.
13   Wuthnow, *After the Baby Boomers*, 133.
14   Ibid., 134.
15   Smith, *Souls in Transition*, 136.
16   Ibid., 252.
17   Ibid., 253.

Chapter Four

1   Mitchell Landsberg, "Young Less Affiliated Not Less Believing," *The Columbian*, February 11, 2010, sec. D.
2   Robert Wuthnow, *After the Baby Boomers: How Twenty- and Thirty-Somethings Are Shaping the Future of American Religion* (Princeton, NJ: Princeton University Press), 168.
3   Ibid., 168.
4   Ibid.
5   Christian Smith. *Souls in Transition: The Religious and Spiritual Lives of Emerging Adults* (New York: Oxford University Press), 141.
6   Ibid.
7   Ibid.
8   Landsberg, sec. D.
9   Pew Forum on Religion and Public Life, "Religion among the Millenials," http://pewforum.org/Age/Religion-Among-the-Millennials.aspx.
10   Smith, *Souls in Transition*, 141.
11   Pew Forum on Religion and Public Life.
12   Smith, 141.

13   Pew Forum on Religion and Public Life.
14   Smith, *Souls in Transition*, 107.
15   Sharon Parks, *The Critical Years: The Young Adult Search for a Faith to Live By* (New York: Harper and Row), 100.
16   Landsberg, sec. D.
17   Pew Forum on Religion and Public Life.
18   Ibid.
19   Ibid.
20   Smith, *Souls in Transition*, 112.
21   Wuthnow, *After the Baby Boomers*, 65.
22   Ibid.
23   Smith, *Souls in Transition*, 112.
24   Ibid., 141.
25   Ibid.
26   Ibid., 214.
27   Ibid., 230.
28   Ibid., 141.
29   Ibid. , 282.
30   Bruce Hunsberger and L. B. Brown, "Religious Socialization, Apostasy, and the Impact of Family Background," *Journal of the Scientific Study of Religion*, 23 (1984), 239-251.
31   Dean Hoge, B Johnson, and D Luidens, "Determinants of Church Involvement and Young Adults Who Grew up in Presbyterian Churches," *Journal of the Scientific Study of Religion*, 32 (1993), 109-130.
32   Jeffrey Jensen Arnett, *Emerging Adulthood: The Winding Road from the Late Teens through the Twenties*, 175.
33   David Caplovitz and Fred Sherrow, *The Religious Dropouts: Apostasy among College Graduates* (Beverly Hills, CA: Sage, 1977).
34   Smith, *Souls in Transition*, 232.
35   Ibid., 214.
36   Ibid., 150.
37   John Ortberg, *Faith and Doubt* (Grand Rapids, MI: Zondervan, 2008), 24.
38   Brian Simmons, "Framing Christian Apostasy in Online Discussion Board Posts," paper presented at the Annual Convention of the Western States Communication Association, February 2009.
39   Smith, *Souls in Transition*, 237.
40   John Wilson and Darren E. Sherkat, "Returning to the Fold," *Journal of the Scientific Study of Religion*, 33 (1994), 148-161.

Chapter Five

1   Jeffrey Arnett, *Emerging Adulthood: The Winding Road from the Late Teens through the Twenties* (New York: Oxford University Press, 2004), 173.
2   Ibid., 172.
3   Bob Altemeyer, "The Decline of Organized Religion in Western Civilization," *International Journal for the Psychology of Religion*, 2 (2004), 77-89.
4   Christian Smith, *Souls in Transition: The Religious and Spiritual Lives of Emerging Adults* (New York: Oxford University Press, 2004), 141-142.
5   Ibid., 142.
6   Spiro Zodhiates, *The Hebrew-Greek Key Study Bible* (Chattanooga, TN: AMG Publishers, 1996), 1611.

7   Kent Schaffer, "Top Reasons for Attending Church," http://www. churchrelevance. com/qa-top-reasons-for-church-attendance/.

8   Ethan Watters, *Urban Tribes: A Generation Redefines Friendships, Family and Commitment* (London: Bloomsbury, 2003).

9   Robert Wuthnow, *After the Baby Boomers: How Twenty- and Thirty-Somethings Are Shaping the Future of American Religion* (Princeton, NJ: Princeton University Press, 2007), 118.

10   Smith, *Souls in Transition*, 52.

11   Christian Smith, *Soul Searching: The Religious and Spiritual Lives of American Teenagers* (New York: Oxford University Press, 2005), 70.

12   Andrew Santella, "The Church Search: Why American Churchgoers Like to Shop Around," http://www.slate.com/id/2211937, February 17, 2009.

13   Wuthnow, *After the Baby Boomers*, 116.

14   Ibid.

15   Ibid., 115.

16   Smith, *Souls in Transition*, 233.

17   Wuthnow, *After the Baby Boomers*, 68.

18   Ibid., 68.

Chapter Six

1   Robert Wuthnow, *After the Baby Boomers: How Twenty- and Thirty-Somethings are Shaping the Future of American Religion* (Princeton, NJ: Princeton University Press, 2007), 17.

2   Ibid., 55.

3   Ibid., 52.

4   Ibid., 62.

5   Jeffrey Arnett, *Emerging Adulthood: The Winding Road from the Late Teens through the Twenties* (New York: Oxford University Press, 2004), 75.

6   Ibid., 97.

7   Ibid., 100.

8   Ibid., 103.

9   Tara Parker Pope, *For Better: The Science of a Good Marriage* (New York: Dutton, 2010).

10   Ibid., 100.

11   William S. Aquilino, "Family Relationships and Support Systems in Emerging Adulthood," in *Emerging Adults in America: Coming of Age in the 21st Century*, ed. Jeffrey Jensen Arnett and Jennifer Lynn Tanner (New York: American Psychological Association, 2006), 202.

12   Eva Lefkowitz and Meghan Gillen, "Sex Is Just a Normal Part of Life: Sexuality in Emerging Adulthood," in *Emerging Adults in America*, 237.

13   Ibid., 238.

14   Ibid.

15   Arnett, *Emerging Adulthood*, 88.

16   Lefkowitz and Gillen, 239.

17   Arnett, *Emerging Adulthood*, 73-74.

18   Carolyn McNamara Barry and Stephanie D. Madsen, "Friends and Friendships in Emerging Adulthood," in *Changing Sea: The Changing Spirituality of Emerging Adults Project*, http://www.changingsea.org/barry.htm.

19   Koji Ueno and Rebecca Adams, "Adult Friendship: A Decade in Review," in *Close Relationships: Function, Form and Processes*, eds. Patricia Noeller and Judith Feeney (New York: Psychology Press, 2006), 151-169.

20   Christian Smith, *Souls in Transition: The Religious and Spiritual Lives of Emerging Adults* (New York: Oxford University Press, 2009), 129.
21   Ibid., 130.
22   Wuthnow, *After the Baby Boomers* 118.
23   Ibid., 118.
24   Smith, *Souls in Transition*, 131.
25   Sharon Parks, *The Critical Years: The Young Adult Search for a Faith to Live By* (New York: Harper and Row, 1986), 200.

Chapter Seven

1   Jeffrey Arnett, *Emerging Adulthood: The Winding Road from the Late Teens through the Twenties* (New York: Oxford University Press, 2004), 119.
2   Ibid., 140.
3   "Debunking the Myths of American College Culture," *Yale Herald Online*, http://yaleherald.com/archive/xxxii/09.07.01/opinion/p9vider.html, September 7, 2001.
4   Christian Smith, *Souls in Transition: The Religious and Spiritual Lives of Emerging Adults* (New York: Oxford University Press, 2009), 54.
5   Arnett, *Emerging Adulthood*, 122.
6   Ibid., 126.
7   Tom Petty, "Tom Petty Quotes," http://thinkexist.com/quotation/you_have_four_years_to_be_irresponsible_here/346270.html, accessed September 28, 2010.
8   Ibid., 284.
9   William S. Aquilino, "Family Relationships and Support Systems in Emerging Adulthood," in *Emerging Adults in America: Coming of Age in the 21st Century*, ed. Jeffrey Jensen Arnett and Jennifer Lynn Tanner (New York: American Psychological Association, 2006), 195.
10   Henry Weschler and Toben F. Nelson, "What We Have Learned from the Harvard School of Public Health College Alcohol Study: Focusing Attention on College Student Alcohol Consumption and the Environmental Conditions That Promote It," *Journal of Studies on Alcohol and Drugs*, 69 (2008): 488.
11   Susan Specher and Elaine Hatfield, "Pre-Marital Sexual Standards among U.S. College Students: Comparison with Russian and Japanese Students," *Archives of Sexual Behavior*, 3 (1996): 263.
12   Smith, *Souls in Transition*, 215.
13   Flavil Yeakley, "A Preliminary Report on Research Conducted for the Christian Higher Education Foundation," Harding University, Searcy, Arkansas, 2007.
14   Stella Y. Ma, "The Christian College Experience and the Development of Spirituality among Students," *Christian Higher Education*, 2 (2003): 237.
15   Robert M. Gonyea and George D. Kuh., *Independent Colleges and Student Engagement: Do Religious Affiliation and Institutional Type Matter?* (Bloomington, IN: Center for Post-Secondary Research, 2006).
16   Yeakley, "A Preliminary Report on Research Conducted for the Christian Higher Education Foundation."
17   Smith, *Souls in Transition*, 284.
18   David Caplovitz and Fred Sherrow, *The Religious Drop-Outs: Apostasy among College Graduates* (Beverly Hills, CA: Sage, 1977).
19   Ernest Pascarella and Patrick Terenzini, *How College Affects Students: A Third Decade of Research* (Hoboken, NJ: Jossey-Bass, 2005).

20   Jenny Lee, "Religion and College Attendance: Change Among Students," *Review of Higher Education*, 25 (2002): 380.

21   Jeremy Uecker, Mark Regnerus, and Margaret Vaaler, "Losing My Religion: The Social Sources of Religious Decline in Early Adulthood," *Social Forces*, 85 (4) (2007): 24.

Chapter Eight

1   Jennifer Lynn Tanner, "Recentering During Emerging Adulthood: A Critical Turning Point in Life Span Human Development," in *Emerging Adults in America: Coming of Age in the 21st Century*, ed. Jeffrey Jensen Arnett and Jennifer Lynn Tanner (New York: American Psychological Association, 2006), 30-31.

2   Suzanne Bartle-Haring, Penny Brucker, and Ellen Hock, "The Impact of Parental Separation Anxiety on Identity Development in Late Adolescence and Early Adulthood," *Journal of Adolescent Research*, 17 (2002): 439-450.

3   William Aquilino, "Family Relationships and Support Systems in Emerging Adulthood," in *Emerging Adults in America: Coming of Age in the 21st Century*, ed. Jeffrey Jensen Arnett and Jennifer Lynn Tanner (New York: American Psychological Association, 2006), 195.

4   Brad E. Sachs, *Emptying the Nest: Launching Your Young Adult toward Success and Self-Reliance* (New York: Palgrave MacMillan, 2010).

5   Joan Atwood, editor, *Family Scripts* (London: Taylor and Francis, 1996).

6   Anna Marie Sturniolo, "I Demand a Rewrite: When a Child Does Not Fit Your Script," in. Joan Atwood, ed., *Family Scripts*, 101-114.

7   Jeffrey Jensen Arnett, *Emerging Adulthood: The Winding Road from the Late Teens through the Twenties*, (New York: Oxford University Press, 2004), 71.

8   Deborah Tannen, *You're Wearing That: Understanding Mothers and Daughters in Conversation* (New York: Ballantine, 2006).

9   Judith S. Dubas and Anne C. Peterson, "Geographical Distance from Parents and Adjustment during Adolescence and Young Adulthood," *New Directions for Child Development*, 17 (1996): 3-19.

10   Christian Smith, *Souls in Transition: The Religious and Spiritual Lives of Emerging Adults* (New York: Oxford University Press, 2009), 43.

11   Christian Smith, *Soul Searching: The Religious and Spiritual Lives of American Teenagers* (New York: Oxford University Press, 2005).

12   Smith, *Souls in Transition*, 128.

13   Leslie A. Baxter, *Relating: Dialogues and Dialectics* (New York: Guilford Press, 1996).

14   Deborah Tannen, *I Only Say This Because I Love You: How The Way We Talk Can Make or Break Family Relationships Throughout Our Lives* (New York: Random House, 2001), xix.

15   Arnett, *Emerging Adulthood*, 48.

16   Frances Goldscheider and Calvin Goldscheider, *The Changing Transition to Adulthood: Leaving and Returning to Home* (Thousand Oaks, CA: Sage,1999), 26.

17   Ibid., 28.

18   Julie DaVanzo and Frances Goldscheider, "Coming Home Again: Returns to the Parental Homes of Young Adults," *Population Studies*, 44 (1990): 249.

19   Caryl Rusbult, "Understanding Responses to Dissatisfaction in Close Relationships: The Exit, Voice, Loyalty, and Neglect Model," in *Conflict Between People and Groups: Causes, Processes, and Resolutions*, eds. Stephen Worchel and Jeffry Simpson (Chicago: Nelson-Hall, 1993), 30-59.

20   John Wilson and Darren Sherkat, "Returning to the Fold," *Journal for the Scientific Study of Religion*, 33(1994): 148-161.